The Emotions In Life

A Book of Poems

and Verse

By :

Peter Köhl

Cover Design by

Eclips Graphics

of Pincourt, Qc.

Cover Photo by:

Peter Köhl

Note for Librarians: A cataloguing record for this book is available from Library and Archives
Canada at www.collectionscanada.ca/amicus/index-e.html
ISBN 1-4251-0163-1

Printed in Victoria, BC, Canada. Printed on paper with minimum 30% recycled fibre.
Trafford's print shop runs on "green energy" from solar, wind and other environmentally-friendly power sources.

Offices in Canada, USA, Ireland and UK

Book sales for North America and international:
Trafford Publishing, 6E–2333 Government St.,
Victoria, BC V8T 4P4 CANADA
phone 250 383 6864 (toll-free 1 888 232 4444)
fax 250 383 6804; email to orders@trafford.com
Book sales in Europe:
Trafford Publishing (UK) Limited, 9 Park End Street, 2nd Floor
Oxford, UK OX1 1HH UNITED KINGDOM
phone +44 (0)1865 722 113 (local rate 0845 230 9601)
facsimile +44 (0)1865 722 868; info.uk@trafford.com
Order online at:
trafford.com/06-1920

10 9 8 7 6 5 4

" The Emotions In Life "

A Book of Poems and Verse by *Peter Köhl*

This is a Collection of *Ideas*, *Experiences* and *Thoughts*, which are part of everyone's experiences, captured by the eye and ear of all and put on paper by Peter.

Some of the verses are life's experiences and others are dreams of what those experiences should be, if and when the ideal situation should occur.

One has to be sensitive to the changes in expression, to see the variations in feelings expressed by a person in many differing situations.

In life, we have to be willing to express those feelings, for relationships to be nourished, and many times we are hesitant to make ourselves vulnerable by expressing our- selves, and in showing those feelings, which are so impor- tant in life.

This group of poems shows my interpretations of what some of those feelings, or expressions of feelings, are like.

There are many people whom I have consulted, and who have inspired me to express these words and feelings and to put them on paper in a form with which I am comfortable in using; **Poetry,** to be shared with others.

To all of these friends, I wish to show my great appreciation.

I am one of those people who came from Europe in the 50's, and had to adapt to the change in school system. I spent many months, which seemed like boring times, as the material covered was a repeat of what I had already studied, just in another language. This time let me day-dream, letting my mind wander and giving me a chance to write at an early age. But a boy writing poetry was not condoned, one was called a " Sissy ", so all of the early work was crumpled and thrown into the " Waste Basket."

It was one of those crumpled pieces of paper, which caught the eye of my teacher, who picked it out and asked me to "Stay after School". Alas! I had been found to be day-dreaming and would be reprimanded for such deeds. But this was not so, as the teacher just complimented me and said I should NOT throw such things away, but I should do them at home, and concentrate at school.

From that time on, I had not kept any papers until 1969 when I was invited to **Deanna's** graduation ceremony from the School of Nursing. I wanted to write a special message for this Special Young Lady, and the result was " A Message To A Graduate "

It was another 14 years before I kept any other writings. In the late 80's, I again decided to put my thoughts and dreams and impressions to paper. Then in the mid 90's, I put together a set of poems for my nephew's Engagement and Wedding. Since then I have kept on writing, not only for the sake of writing, but using poems as a way of expressing myself on sensitive topics. It was easier to give a sheet of paper with a poem than to say to a person, that which might have made me blush, or to open up to a special friend and be afraid of not coming across properly.

Writing poems, for me, was a way of verbally painting scenes and emotions to paper, and later on, I learned how to recite these poems with almost the same conveyance of feeling and emotion.

This may not be so convincing when the subject matter is more emotional, and one has to fear moments of anxiety or sheer panic of Blushing myself Crimson, as some of the Poems are a trite deep on the amorous intonations.

These poems are my expression of feelings of, and about, the events in a normal life cycle, with a strong resemblance to my own life's experience, and those of many others. It is with pleasure I wish to share these words which many people feel, but are also a little too shy to express.

I sincerely wish that the readers reflect on their own past, see the present and envision their future situations in this collection of writings.

To the many people who have inspired me, shaped my feelings and had the patience to support me in my attempts to express myself, I give Heartfelt Thanks.

" Individually you know who you are! "

Peter Köhl

About the Author:

Peter is a man of many talents with eagerness to participate in, discover and enjoy new experiences. He has a deep passion and respect for nature and the outdoors. His love for travel, music, photography and dance are important elements in his daily personal and social life.

When presented, he will grasp the opportunity to provide a helping hand, render some advice or even jump in and actively participate in a group discussion on whatever topic is at hand and make new friends (develop new relationships)

Peter is sensitive, caring, devoted to his family and loyal and faithful to his friends, as many of us can attest.
On numerous occasions, he has touched the hearts of many with a selection of poetry or prose he presented, which was perfectly suited for that special occasion.

Peter is articulate and creative; his collection of works manifests his sensitivity, his feelings and reveals his innermost thoughts and self. In verse, he captures not only his own serious moments, his deep, personal thoughts, emotions and experiences but also mundane daily experiences and occurrences.
He questions and reflects on thoughts or feelings that others might overlook or take for granted and uses verse to express his feelings that might be difficult to express verbally.

The poems in this book are an example of Peter's ability to observe and capture the expressions and feelings of others and to share these with all who have received poems in the past and now with those who will read these selections.

Frank Biringer.

This book contains *Poems* and *Verse* and some
pictures of *People* and *Objects* which have
affected some of my
emotions and which influence people to reflect
upon their own Lives & Feelings.

Some of these people are *Friends* who
have helped me,
Musicians who have inspired me, and *Objects*
which are dear to one's Heart.

All these above
are the things which keep me inspired and
certainly some of these will also inspire you.

Pictures will be featured in the center of the book
and references made to some via photo numbers.
Sketches are placed beside some poems to
complement the words within those poems.

Emotions: In life there are many: Some we share, and most we try to hide. Happiness, Elation, Longing and Pain as well as Sadness and Loss. In this collection, I try to share some of the emotions I have observed in friends, family, witnessed in others and also experienced myself.

> **They are feelings *ALL* of us have, or have had on various occasions; now, in the past, and will have in the future.**

My First Recorded Poem

A Message to a Graduate

Chapter 1: Friendship, Blossoming to ... Much More

Chapter 2: The Dare

Chapter 6: The Parting

A Thorn
A Hummingbird
The Silvery Moon

Chapter 7: Tribulation, Sadness and Health

Pain
The Ravages of Time
How Do I Speak ?
Anger -- At Me or Because of Me ?
Which is My Strength ?
The Little Vampire
Is Life a Duel ?
Night Time Sounds in Room 281 D
The Day She Came to Visit
Memory

Chapter 8: Nourishment of Body and Soul

Friends in Music
My Glass of Wine
Musik Governs My Day
A Pause, Tea Break or Coffee if you Please
A Thought When Cutting Onions or
        Other Slippery Things
Grappa
Voice
Music… and Song, Are a Voice in the Night
Cream Cheese with Bacon
Waffles and Waffles
The Sandman
Rain

Chapter 9:   Retirement

Chapter 10:   Leisure and Sports

Chapter 11:   Family

Chapter 12:   The Word

Chapter 13:   Last Voyage and Departure

Poetry Credits, Influences and Inspiration:

Thank You

A Message to a Graduate

These three long years were long indeed
So long they were, you learned the creed,
That time is here to follow the road;
You sought to find three years behind.

The road goes on around the bend
Then straightens out to never end.
It twists and turns in its long course
But never cuts from its source.

These same three years that you have spent,
Your parents to you their patience lent,
To see you leave, your home to part;
So that, in time your own life to start.

The time has come for you to part
These friends; who also have learned they must start
To do the work which time has brought,
And fulfill the duties you have sought.

May 1969

Chapter 1: Friendship, . . . Blossoming to Much More

A Friend
Kiss
Sparkle
Love
Palpitations
A Rose
A Vase

A Friend

A Friend is a person,
Who wishes to listen
To tales we wish to tell,
A sounding board for our ideas.

A friend is also
That shoulder which we
Sometimes need, to share our burden
Which we carry.

A friend is that
Soul who can console us,
When our inner selves seek solace;
And pry us from our shell.

A friend is a person
Who shares his happiness,
And thrills, with others
Who have need to share.

A friend is that person
Who, also may require
Our contact; oft times rare.
To share the load,

To reminisce the laughter,
The youth, and adventure,
Of having endured, and shared
A friendship.

January 3, 1995

A Kiss

A Kiss is but
A gentle brush,
The faintest touch
Upon her Lips.

A soft and tender touch
With which to show,
Kindness and Adoration
For the soul, contained within.

It should be given, ever so soft,
That Down would weigh much more
And glide so silently,
To contact rosy, parted Lips.

Ardently we bring our Lips together
Our Passions wish to almost crush;
To bring the weight of deep Emotions,
And deposit on her Tender Lips.

This Kiss should touch not only Lips,
The whole Body be included.
Forget not all the zones
Which flame from softest touch.

Such Kiss can also be a Duel
Between two Lovers, as they spar,
Two Tongues engaged in Ritual Battle,
To conquer higher Passion.

A Kiss is a bonding of two
Loving Souls, whose Bodies
Flame, with feelings burning with
Temptation, just Awakened by a Kiss.

A Kiss can also heal a Wound,
Upon the Hand or Soul.
And Mend a broken Heart,
By Sealing with a Kiss.

September 3, 1995

A Sparkle

This is a light
Within your eyes
When you smile at me
For whatever I might have done.

It is a twinkle in the
Depth of your eye,
When somehow
I have pleased you.

Awakened is a
Radiance of emotions,
Spilled out by this pleasure
To alight in your eyes.

This glitter, thus shines
To show, in your ways
And your deeds,
However you try not.

Such sparkles are
Contagious, and affect
Those around you,
Even me.

Be it Sparkle or Twinkle
Let it stay in your eyes
And let it light up
A smile.

September 4, 1994

Love

How can I recognize
This feeling, which I cannot describe,
This trembling, flutter of my pulse ?
Is it Love ?

Is it the Flicker of your Eyes?
When you look upon me
With that longing look,
And daring smile?

I sense the quickening of your Breath,
As I approach your side.
A Sparkle shines from your eyes,
As you try, not to give yourself away.

Can this be something which
We dare not, call love?
Words which exactly describe the
Feelings, which abound in our Hearts.

This hesitation in your words,
This wanting ... waiting ... silent Plea,
Does it mean there are
Some feelings, which I dare

Construe to mean, I know not why,
That I cannot see, through the
Blindness in my hinter Eye,
That there is Love ?

The quiet deeds, and subtle glance
Are signs of bubbling feelings
Which we try not to verbalize, for fear
They may be called . . . some word as " Love. "

Why do men hide these feelings,
While women wish to share?
To recognize the words, which are
In both our hearts. Is this " Love " ?

June, 1995

Palpitations

This is a trembling of the Heart
When sighting someone,
Or something, which has caught your eye,
And stirred some memory.

The recollection of these thoughts,
Causes Heart and Breath a-beating
To show itself, as blush and glow
Your face thus flushed with colour.

Can this be a sign of feelings deep?
Or just a wish to share
The feelings, which a comrade finds,
In words she reads somewhere?

With these few words in this small poem
Your thoughts be stirred to
Acknowledge, that words are there
To share with all, and feelings also.

Was this your heart, which fluttered?
Or that of comrade, and you've noticed,
And caused you such great joy
To share with her these Blushes?

December 19, 1995

A Rose

A Rose we search, with petals soft as Velvet
Whose colour may be red, or pink,
Or any combination which we find,
When we choose this flower of the Heart.

Why are its petals such a prize,
Which we give to Mademoiselle?
To gather this flower, one must be brave;
The thorns, great pain can bring.

Is the ardour of the hope so great,
That we must risk these tiny prickles,
To show our courage to attain
A smile; or perhaps an invitation?

May it be friendship which we wish to nurture,
Or love we come to seek
When with a Rose, we pledge our feeling?
Would the colour of the flower make a difference,
If only one were found?

Why is it Red, which pleases her?
Does Passion have some say,
Or Pink, whose tone is softer,
Bring hope and stirring emotions?

If white is brought, will she forgive
What we had brought upon us,
This pain to settle in our hearts?
This Rose, so delicate in brightness.

Not bright, like light or snow, but shade of Ivory,
A purity of softness like her hand or cheek,
When holding her in light embrace
Likened to handling petals pure.

If longing is her pain to bear,
A yellow rose she will find.
To soothe her aching heart,
Till you come back again.

Now to the Florist I do venture,
In search of blossom, for to bring,
As Wild ones are not close at hand,
Winter season will not allow.

I find one, which I pray
Will please her, for the courage I had shown
Not for the thorn, but Trip to Flower store
With hope, and anticipation.

December 18 1999
(Picture # 2 A Rose)

A Vase

In this vase you will find,
Not emptiness, but space,
For all those unknown
Joys and Fears.

It should be filled with Hopes
Which certainly, you will wish to Treasure,
And Dreams of all ,that can come true,
In life that is before you.

This Vase is neither sealed nor coloured,
So daily you may look inside,
And add if needed, more of wishes
And desires, that you can expect.

This Vase is for you to treasure,
Not just things of the future,
The past, can also hide,
Only to be seen by you.

For it is Transparent, like all
Dreams and Hopes
Which are yours alone,
To hide from all,
But you.

Like the Vase,
Transparent and Empty
Are your Hopes and Fears,
Until you Share and Tell,
What is contained therein.

Your future is in this Vase,
Fill it with Love and Joy.
Look daily, and add to it,
Your Dreams of Life to fulfill.

December 7, 1996

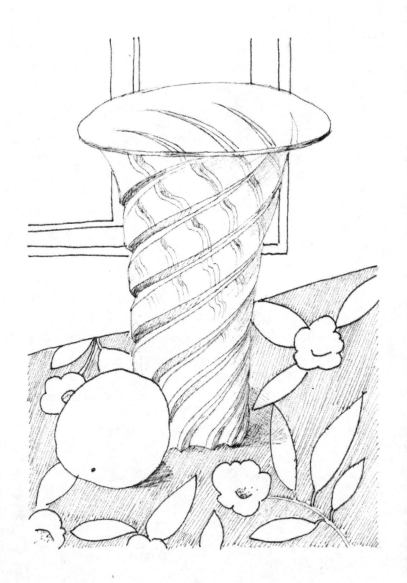

Chapter 2: The Dare

Happy Valentine

A Smile For You Today

Love on Valentine's Day

On This Day I Wander

Heed me, I do Say

Saint Valentine

This Hand

Happy Valentine

On this day, may you wear a Smile,

To brighten up the day, a Smile to make others smile with you,

To carry your day, and ease the load of worries.

A smile to share with others, who may need a smile,

A radiant smile till the day is done.

A smile for me . . . if one is left to spare.

A Smile . . . for Valentine.

February 13, 2001

A Smile For You Today

. . . .
.

A smile for you today,
  Will make the rain go away.
It will part the clouds,
  So the Sun can shine your way.

It will brighten your outlook on life,
  When things have gotten in your way.
Smile for me, and you will have a great day,
  For Tomorrow you will then set aside that strife.

Smile, it makes you feel great, and more youthful today.

August 13, 2002

Love on Valentine's Day

Love is the joy, the companionship and the laughter we can share, the emotions and the feelings of longing and of delight when we meet.

It is the sharing of our precious time in many of the things we do. Love is also the glances and smiles of chiding and support . . . in a harmonious and thoughtful discourse.

The looks and feeling which are evoked by our actions and words, are manifestations of that small word.

It is also a sharing of tender moments of rapture and passion as we cling to each other in loving embrace.

It is the soft little kisses we steal now and then, when we meet for our dances and dinners, here and there.

This is what we celebrate on this Valentine's Day.

For my Love on this Day

February 14, 2002

On this day I wander,
To visit this little Lass
I do not know what card to bring,
As I cannot find the proper words,
So maybe, for her I should sing.

I travel on this day, so special it is said,
On Valentine to see her,
To see what she will say,
For I have work to do for her
Any maybe time to play.

Have a very, Happy Valentine

February, 2003

Heed me, I do Say

Heed me, Read me, but do not lead me astray!
Heed me, when I ask, " Shall we romp in the hay?"
Heed me when I search your eyes, and ask by my side for
you to stay.
Lead me to your loft by the bay.

We scramble up gingerly to the head of the stairway
And at my side, on satin sheets you choose then to lay.
And in our throes and passion to the Lord we shall pray
That such moments like this forever we'll play.

When sated we'll sit by the fireside and look at the bay
Or go down to beachside and swim in the fray,
When refreshed we will love again, and I won't say NAY
As you lead me back to your loft by the Bay.

December 10, 2005

Saint Valentine

He was a Saint,
With Heart and Soul,
To spread the Word
Of Attraction between Boy and Girl.

In aid to his deeds,
Cupid close at his side.
Sent an Arrow
Of Rapture to target ahead.

His aim was good,
For the Hearts were pierced,
And Feelings of Love,
In couples did gleam.

Many people have since,
Named Valentine to Saint,
Inspiration to Lovers
He surely did paint.

February 6, 1996

This Hand

Is this the hand that guides me,
Or holds me when I need,
Your strength to lead me through my trials,
While in Autumn collecting seed ?

This hand it holds me when I tremble,
It smoothes my ruffled mane.
It reassures me all is well, and will
Guide me, and my fears will still.

This hand, it nestles in my palm,
When tenderly it searches,
To hold, to grasp, for comfort and care
Like mine, it also seeks its share.

Was it so long it held mine, till
We both began to tremble,
As we groped for feelings in our hearts
And our bodies strained to get their fill?

I lay my palm so gently to your cheek
With fingers pause . . . to feather by your lip
Then feel a quiver in your breath
While your dreamy eyes look into mine.

This hand has stirred some feelings deep,
And pulled a tender string,
Which set the heart a' pounding loud
As we yearn for passion to reap.
Only then we realize, that love is such a fleeting thing.

Take my hand . . . If not as lover,
Then take it as a friend.

May 23, 2002

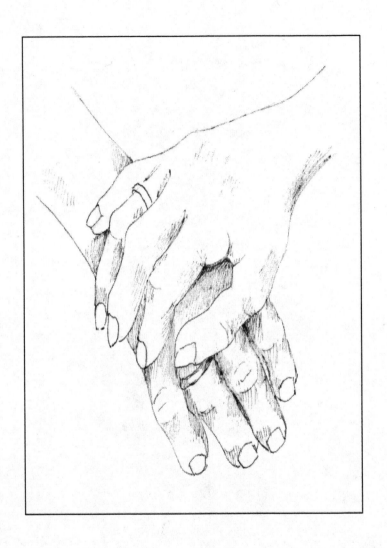

Chapter 3: Start of Passion

A Caress

Beauty

A Gem

My Love, Will You make Love to Me ? ((Song))

Passion

A Caress

This is something which we wish
To receive from time to time,
From the one with whom we hope
To share . . . a long and tender moment.

We also wish to give in return
This same soft touch, to nurture
A delight in senses, of Body and Soul,
And renew the bond between us.

This soft touch can be felt and dealt
So gently with our hands,
Let eyes also partake,
In warm soft gaze, and glance.

With such a feeling,
We will languish and delight
Our emotions and our souls,
When receiving such caress.

A gentle stroke from soft hand
To frill with Hair and Cheek,
To pass over lips and brow,
And entice a kiss upon those lips.

A caress with these lips can be
More tender than the lightest
Of the fingers, or gentlest
Embrace we dare to use,
For pleasure just to see.

The contact at our meeting
When first your hand I touched,
Enflamed a feeling in my soul,
It tore my breath apart.

May I caress you with mine eyes,
My hands and lips included ?
Without your consent I would die,
Then my heart would be secluded.

October 9, 2000.

Beauty

Beauty is a word, which describes
A Young Girl or Woman, whose appearance
Makes one's head turn about,
To see if eyes have deluded me,
Or if the apparition still is there.
I blink my eye, if in fact it is beholding.

Oh yes, she moved, she caught my eye
And peaked my curiosity.
Where had this Lass been hiding?
Or was I hidden from this earth so long,
That I had lost touch with reality, of beauty
Almost everywhere, and I was blind to see?

Now this one caused my head to stir,
A beauty, of design by sculptured hand,
The Lord had created a specimen rare.
She wears no paint, to hide her charm,
Or hide some imperfection,
But shows a vibrant natural charm.
Her head held high with shoulders back, exuding health and aura,
To make a man wonder why he has not seen her before.

What do I see, in my beleaguered state,
When finally introduced I am, to this young
Mademoiselle, as she stole my breath away?
A Dream? An Apparition? No, just a sample of what beauty
Should be, in flesh and living form.

For this old man, who has been so secluded, by choice his own,
This chance encounter wakes him out of mental Hibernation,
And rekindles all feelings, which have been left to die,
From pains of years gone by, which pierced the heart like lance.
This introduction, by a friend who did a good deed,
To this young beauty before my eye, leaves me in dream-like trance.

We talk, we dance, and talk some more and evening is almost over,
but just before I take my leave, I present her with some verse,
That speaks much more than my voice can say.
Of what my thoughts of nature are, and poems of words for giving,
To give of myself, my scattered ideas, of what I see in life.

These poems are a group of words, when inspired I became, I composed
my feelings to this sheet, for to give it to such beauty.
What does she read into these words of mine? Are they much too Personal,
Or will she see, they relate to all, and enjoy the message within?

Will she allow me, my sport to show, in canoe or kayak venture,
And ply with me the waves of lakes, in sunshine of next summer?
Am I asking too much when I know her not, to dream of something,
I've not dared allow to happen?

When camera I sport and wish to compose, an Image of Scenery and
Beauty,
I click at the shutter and freeze the moment for keeping
To compliment the words of poetry and prose,
Which help to describe her beauty.
There is also beauty in verse and in voice, when listening to stories and im-
pressions, of things which are dear to her heart and her soul, and which are
her most likely companions. Her soul she does search and friendship she
seeks.

What is beauty? A friend to behold, in harmony with nature and song,
With a radiant smile, and sparkle of voice and delight.

Behold her and judge for yourself.

October 9, 2000

A Gem

A Gem is this Lady who has made my eyes glisten,
With pride and joy, for finding such prize.
She has polished this rough stone, and mellowed his soul.
And lay by my side, in heavenly throes.

Her eyes shine when I fondle her hair, and play with her fingers
As I travel across her body to awaken a fire.
I cup this breast and fondle the nipple as she's pleading,
Then nibble its scent with a tongue oh so pleasing.

Behold I, the glimmer and sparkle in her eyes,
She does likewise to raise me to heightened longing and strife,
Wishing to quell this flame, with a dip in the well.
As we lose ourselves in passionate bliss.

We search each our souls and our passions let sail,
In the sea of such fountains of love-moistened sweat.
The dew of our loving and heat of our flesh,
Will be sated by gently holding this gem,
For minutes or hours in loving embrace.
I look at the sparkle of this gem in my arms.

Yes, she is a gem to behold, as she shines and sparkles,
With a light oh so bright, and more so when I've loved her,
Then blindingly bright, her eyes shine
With such love in return.

A Rare Gem I have found,

My Awakening Light.

September 2, 2001

My Love, Will You Make Love to Me?

My Love will you make love to me, (Refrain)
While I sing this small refrain ?
My Love will you make love to me,
When walking in the rain ?

I Love you when the sun comes up
I Love you when the sunset glows
My love will you make love to me
Before I go insane, with longing for your tender touch?
Bring to me passion, of ever greater throes, with such
Slender, nimble fingers, as you trace so fine,
So sensual . . . A line, across my tingling spine.

(Refrain)

My Love will you make love to me,
While I write this new refrain?
Will you make love to me,
All night till the morning rain?

I'll hold you in my arms till then,
And keep the drops from you.
At daybreak for a swim we'll spree,
Then race back to shore, to bask and behold
The sun's rays though the myriad of droplets on your skin,
Like tiny prisms . . . a thousand diamonds gleam.

(Refrain)

We'll walk across the sandy beach
In sunshine and in rain,
My Love, I'll make more love to you
In hidden shady glen,
We'll bask in sunrays and shade till then
Making love from twilight, till well after ten.
My love will you make love to me
Forever and again?

(Refrain)

We'll come back now and then again
In Autumn, Winter and Springtime too.
My Love, we'll embrace in love again
Beneath the blankets new.
But not in bed or beach, like summer time.
Instead, at fireside warmth I'll lie,
In loving arms with you.

(Refrain)

A sip of wine with chestnut roast
Beside the roaring flames,
We nibble on the food of love,
While I trace the swell of breast so white
And fondle rosy peak inflamed.
Forever I will do this so,
While making love to you.

(Refrain)

I look upon your rosy cheeks,
They show what we have seen,
And show where we have been today
There's proof, I'd made more love to you,
And you did same to me.
My Love will you make love to me,
And sing with me this new refrain?
While embraced we will remain . . .

March 24, 2002

Passion

I find not love within her bosom
Nor do I find it between her thighs
But see it, simmering, sparkling in her eyes.
Thus I do seek and search so far and near,
And fondle bosom, two spires dear,
In search through forest of pleading sighs,
To find that it was written in her eyes.

I See Passion

A haven, I found amongst those mounds
Topped with turgid Peaks, The colour of Red Wine
And taste the thrill, and chill of Heights attained
When with my lips I taste those Fountains,
Then hear a moan, much louder than my breath
As we languish in Heat and Fever.

I found Passion

I search and fondle, in exploration
Over skin so sensitive, in present state,
To cup those lovely breasts, and fondle Rosy Peaks
Then wander to the Apex of Thighs and Mound,
And forest dense with coarse down.
I search the cleft, with crimson lips,
Lips at the Portals of an entrance to a
Chasm, a Fount of softness to encase my
Manhood, throbbing, unrestrained, as I enter
This realm, this vault of Passion.

Together we fulfil this Passion.

January 29, 2002

Chapter 4: Engagement and Wedding

Patrizia and Martin

A Wedding

Un Matrimonio
  (Wedding Poem Translated to Italian by
          Kathleen Di Genova)

Patrizia and Martin

I wish to you both the very best:

The decision you have made is
A promise of sharing of your
Aspirations and your joys,
And also your strengths.

In every relationship there will be weaknesses,
Which must be accepted with an understanding
That both of you need to acknowledge them,
And only then will you be able to overcome them.

To promise your future
You will need to build an understanding,
A willingness to learn each other's
Handicaps, and to overcome them and
Make them your strengths.

On some occasions you may have doubts
In your abilities, and your judgements.
Both of you should not be too reserved,
Ask for advice, for we may have some words
of experience that can help you both.

Build your future, and share your hopes
And then you will nourish your love.
Life's adventures will test you both,
So do not despair, but learn from this, as
Your life together will be, above all,
A complete compliment to each other.

Bless you both in your commitment
And I wish you a Very Happy Future.

Your Uncle

A Wedding

A Wedding is a Joining on this Special Day,
A Joining in the presence
Of God, and all of us Assembled here.
It is a commitment
To each other, before us all.

This Wedding is an agreement between
Patrizia and Martin
To live their life together,
To share their aspirations
And their dreams.

This joining brings two
Solitary lives together into a
Harmonious sharing of each other's
Laughter, Fears and Joys,

This life as one, should be shared
Yet still you are individual, and need
Time on your own,
Your inner souls to replenish.

With the Lord's help, may your road be
Straight and True,
And your strength be such
To weather the storms which will beset you.

Have the courage to Live your own lives
To not allow others to Deter your ways,
But have the Judgement to
Accept the Advice which others may bestow.

I, along with all present here,
And those who were not able to attend,
Wish to you both, the Very Best.

Your Uncle " Peter "

UN MATRIMONIO

Il matrimonio è unione
in questa giornata speciale,
è una promessa fatta tra voi due
alla presenza di Dio e di noi tutti
riuniti qui.

Questo matrimonio è un accordo tra
Patrizia & Martin,
per vivere le loro vite insieme e
dividere i loro sogni ed aspirazioni.

Quest'unione porta due vite solitarie
insieme, non dimenticando che siete
individui, e come tali avrete bisogno
del vostro tempo, per rifornire le vostre
anime.

Con l'aiuto di Dio, che la vostra strada
sia diritta e vera, e che abbiate la forza
di oltrepassare le tempeste che potranno
presentarsi davanti a voi.

Abbiate il coraggio di vivere la vostra vita,
e di non lasciare agli altri dissuadere le
vostre possibilit..., dovrete avere l'abilit...
d'ascoltare tutti i consigli giudicando solo
quelli di buon senso.

Io, insieme con tutti noi qui, e colui che
non è qui in questo momento, vi auguriamo
un mondo di Gioia e Prosperit...!

June, 1994.
Tui zio " Peter "

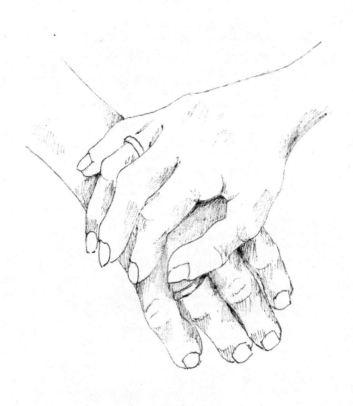

Chapter 5:
Birthdays and Other Occasions

A Birthday Comes just Once a Year

A Little Birdie Told Me

Another Birthday

Is It Your Birthday Today?

Leontine

Dear Monique

Fifteen

Johanna and Eddie

Twenty Five
      (Mary and Frank's 25th Anniversary)

Fifty

Birthdays are a Number

Dear Sheelagh

New Year's Wish 2005

A Birthday comes just Once a Year

For this you should not shed a Tear.

Rejoice the number you've attained,

To Double this: should be your aim.

With Health and Challenge

For those yet to come

This Birthday be a

Special One

Happy Birthday

March 15, 1997

A little Birdie told me
When it twittered in my ear,
A little bitty secret
That you would rather not hear.

The time has come around again
Like every other year,
When all of us will wish to you,
A birthday, oh so dear.

Now this year is a special one
As you have climbed that distant knoll,
You realized that the summit is
Some fifty leagues beyond.

Have a very Happy Birthday

December 5, 2000

Another Birthday

Once again like the annual migration,
the days keep Migrating . . . another notch.

We work at trying not to count the notches,
but the creases in our lives show the notches.
We try to hide from them,
but they find us. We can try to run away from them,
but they run beside us at the same speed.

So the answer is not to run, but Celebrate where we
have come to, the experiences we have learned and lived,
and the notches we have attained.

So I am writing to celebrate with you the experiences
we have shared and the days, months and years,
like the waters that have passed beside us.

Have a Happy Birthday remembering all of those times.

October 9, 2001

Is It Your Birthday Today?

Another Birthday rolls around
   The numbers they just seem to bound
I count the creases around my eyes
   And find they do not tell me lies.
And when I look upon your face
   I see that you are keeping pace.

The will to keep fit, keeps us trim
   And this we do, not just on a Whim,
So that we maintain our youthful form,
   And hear only complaints, coming from our Bones.

So on this day we come to Celebrate
   And bring you wishes, before we're late.
For this we raise our glass of Cheer
   For you have known us for another year.

Happy Birthday

May 22, 2002

Leontine

It seems like Yesterday,
I held this little bundle
And only yesterday when I was
That much younger.

It was but yesterday
In God's Eternal Year
That Leontine was born.
Now, here we are to celebrate again.

From Yesterday until Today
I've lost some youth
And gained some girth
Then found my Hair receding,

While this little bundle changed from little Girl
To striking Lass, and she did grow to be
Young lady, a beauty to behold.
What change from then, till now?

It gives me pleasure to behold
God's Treasures as they change,
From little bundle of Yesterday,
To Woman, of today.

On this, your Birthday,
I wish you the Very Best

April 11, 2000

Dear Monique

Eighteen is a year which all
Young Girls await.
It is a year which says
Legally you are women,
But in your heart you know
You are just another
Day Older.
Do not let the number of the Years
Make you lose track of your youth
As the years will pass all but too fast,
And then you will look back for the youth
Which is no longer, and has slipped by.
Treasure this year as you will
Not see it again in the future
Nor be able to go back to, either.
Enjoy this one and only Eighteenth,
For it also prepares you for the future.

Have a Happy Eighteenth Birthday
And an Exciting Future to come.

Dec 7, 1993

Fifteen

This is a number which
Causes great grief and anxiety for
Every young man, as his Body
Sends mixed messages to the mind.

To say to assert yourself, but
How does one accomplish this?
When the hormones are playing tricks
To the body and mind.

You have temptations, which mind
Cannot decipher as yet,
And body has changes, the voice
Plays quavering tricks to your speech.

This is the playground of youth and young man
To wander between Adult and Boy,
To tempt you to be one,
But the other are still.

You must all travel this route,
Your future to discover,
But rough may the road be
In becoming a man.

Enjoy what is left of this youth,
As a man, your future more rough it will be.
To recapture what is lost,
Will not come about when you are a man.

Enjoy this Fifteen
And have the courage to ask for help,
In answering those questions which
Sure come about.

Happy Birthday.

November 6, 1995

Johanna and Eddie

Twenty-Five years are an achievement,
something to be proud of when you look back and see
how you have grown, the family you have raised, and the
accomplishments you have shared. There may have been
times of sorrow and of hard times, but that was only a test
of your commitment to each other.

The next *Twenty-Five* will be the chance to look
back on how you might have done things differently,
on how you may make it better for yourselves,
while you see your children take the same paths
you took, those *Twenty-Five* years ago.

Be proud of those *Twenty-Five* years as you may
not take them back; you cannot reverse the sad and
happy times. Make the best of the next *Twenty-Five*.

Best Wishes from your friend.

December 18, 1992

Twenty-Five

It was many a year ago
and was called Two-Bits.
It bought you a lot of things,
If you had a few more in your hand.

Two-Bits of years since you have tied the knot,
A new generation has sprung from this union.
Two-Bits of getting used to each other,
With toddlers to get in the way.

Look at them now and
Look way back then,
It was not so long ago,
When Two-Bits an eternity seemed.

Silver it is worth, as the Two-Bits had been,
Which you spent on that lass˙
Long ago, and
She fell for you then as she stands by you now.

Silver you celebrate for a
Part of your life
You've Shared, each other you've nurtured
With love and devotion.

Twenty-five is just half of the next
Quarter century which comes just as fast.
Enjoy it with Health, and Happiness too
For Gold comes at next round,
Twenty-five years from now.

Your Friend

August 1994

Fifty

This is just the
Beginning of another
Half a Century
In which we strive,

To complete the
Things we started
In the First Half,
But never did complete.

This is also the period
When wisdom has beset us,
And things are done with reason
Not just for sake of doing.

Our life has become a pendulum
With challenges overcome,
Now is the time to enjoy
The Pleasures we had set aside,

During the race to mount
The Pinnacle of life,
Only to find, it was just a ridge,
The spire, is yet to come.

Look forward to that distant peak,
And make not haste to get there.
As time will surely race across
The span of life, you'll see.

This Fifty was just half the Journey
The next to be taken in stride,
With laughter and joy
We will attain that peak of

Another Fifty more.

Have a Happy Fiftieth Birthday

October 27, 1996

Birthdays are a Number

When we were young, our Mothers made us remember
At every change of the New Year, of the birthday that is to come.

In nature the creatures do not count, as
The years they are noted in experience they gain.

In children the numbers are counted, as soon as they learn at young age,
In later years, they are noted by the inches in height that they gain.

In nature they are noted in the maturity the creatures attain,
In adolescents it is almost the identical same.
Then at some period of numbers, the ideal partner is found,
And life as a couple, for a lifetime of joy will resound.

The hormones they do flow and the passions they dictate
As the life does continue, in ritual and time,
And children and offspring are brought forth,
From this passing of minutes in blissful refrain.

Now on this Birthday they all came to visit
Their Father, who has attained this grouping of decades;
To fête with him and mother and some friends
By dining and dancing in celebration of numbers attained.

We count not the years, but the experiences we've shared
As we see their children all grown,
With a crop of their own children, counting the years
They have been on their own.

Frank: On this, your Special Birthday, let us all share in this
celebration of the days which have passed.

October 29th, 2004.

Dear Sheelagh

I could not find a flower
Nor could I find a card
For words in cards are not my
Choice, to express what I wish to say.

I sometimes call a little late,
And sometimes not at all,
But this time I wish to make amends,
By calling at the door.

What do I bring? An empty hand!
Some paper there may be,
Of words I wish to share with you,
On this, your special day.

You wish not to remember
The number which it marks,
But days are only passing thoughts,
Of all those days gone by.

For this occasion, a Flower I do offer
To celebrate with you
And all your family by your side,
The times, which slipped us by.

I wish you a very Happy Birthday.

Sunday January 16, 2000

New Year's Wish
2005

May your year be worry-free,
and give you time to sit under the tree,
to collect your thoughts, and to smile a lot,
At Festive meal around the dinner Pot.
So enjoy your loved ones throughout the year,
so please; You should not shed a tear,
For after this there is another year.

If one were to look back, way too far,
then I'd say we set the door ajar,
To haunt the future with last year's pain
and keep us from the New Year's Gain.

Now, frill not with the wanted gifts,
and toss away the shopping list.
Make your Christmas like of old again,
with Family you sit and sing some refrain.

Come visit, if it pleases you, or
Welcome guests who wish to chat with you.
So tip a glass and make your wish
and let them stay if they had a few
and thus they'll help with cleaning the dish.

So, let your Christmas be Merry and Free
then in distant years you'll remember sitting by the tree,
and if by year's end you're still fine,
come back and join us when we dine.

SO! Raise this Glass to the Outgoing Year,
And wash the New One in, with another Cheer.

Saturday, January 1, 2005

Chapter 6: The Parting

A Thorn

A Hummingbird

The Silvery Moon

A Thorn

Do not weep for me
For I cannot be,
The man whom you had thought
That I would be.

Sometime I may be
Just a thorn,
For your heart, I may have torn
By some deed, I still don't know.

Some time I am only pain,
For I know not what a strain.
That a friendship can attain,
When we do not wish to gain

Closer ties to one we have
Befriended, using charm or subtle glance
Only to find, that we must take a stance,
Because our feelings can not bear the chance,

That we fear, it can be true,
Our tender souls have
Come to cherish,
That sweet smile, so dear and devilish.

Deprived my senses of all longing,
For I might become entranced
By your Song and fond Caress,
And my heart may then confess,

What your heart would surely wish to learn,
My tranquility would burn with
Pain and Sorrow, sense of reject
Because I could not come to terms,

With what you had thought
That there might be,
Future for us in some way,
If my heart with yours might stay.

Inner hurt and fears of past,
Will forever burn and last
For my heart to respond and show
Laughter, joy and answers slow.

Was there ever a tender moment?
Yes, and feelings more than words can tell.
I am not of Stone, or Ash
As the Flames can surge from

Glowing embers, which I hide from
Fearsome winds, or thoughts
And rain of questions, which I fear
Expose my warmth to danger near.

Danger, may just be perception
Of the unknown, a misconception
Of caress and displayed affection,
Towards my deeds and tender person.

Be it lack of strength, or weakness
In resolve and drive, and prowess,
For as man, I ought to strive
In search of lover, or just friend.

Is my silence such a strain,
And my word of such great pain,
That our friendship should be rendered
To a thought and memory.

My heart also has been hurt
By these feelings, words and looks
Which have come between us,
Like the bush wherein the Thorn.

Can there be such thing as friend,
When you search for more affection,
Which I cannot learn to show,
As I am but just a mortal?

In our feelings and expression
You will show and I will hide,
Heart and soul will be affected,
By the piercing of this Thorn.

March 31, 1997

A Hummingbird

A Hummingbird is free to fly
Just like the Butterfly.
When flower wilts or
Glass comes in-between.

The nectar of the Love we shared
Is now so weak and lost
That waiting for the newest blossom
Which has not come to bloom,

Will leave this Hummingbird
In feeble state, for nourishment to search
When flower is not open,
And glass comes in between.

This glass is trust and fear,
Of giving of myself to you
In light of pain which had been cast,
Between our hearts so soon.

Why wait till then, but set your wings
And fly to freedom now,
As time will only wither bloom
That is behind glass door.

Yes! There was love,
Hidden behind a smoky pane,
And I could not, just clear the glass,
Nor open window pane.

This flower is not food for you
So fly, and fly to search.
For lingering will not heal this wound
And time too precious for delay.

I hold you not,
Be free of me, for Pain to ease
with time, A voyage for a quest to find
And leave this flower behind.

May gentle winds
Assist your flight, for happiness to find.

August 22, 1997

The Silvery Moon

I see the shining moon
Under a clear night sky
I see the shining silvery moon.
Why? Are you leaving so soon?

I look to see if there is a face,
Looking back to earth at me
Perhaps I am just dreaming
Of what I thought there just might be.

I see the bright cherubic face look down at me,
As I linger by that lonesome tree.
I thought I heard the whisper of your voice,
Or perhaps it was the sigh of wind, through leaves above.

A chill sweeps over me, like an Omen I foresee
That you are not content with me,
Because I eluded a commitment with thee
And this the wind had whispered to me.

As I look upon the lonely moon
He shines his light upon my path.

Why have you left so soon?

December 22, 2004

Chapter 7: Tribulation, Sadness and Health

Pain

The Ravages of Time

How Do I Speak ?

Anger - At Me or Because of Me ?

Which is my Strength ?

The Little Vampire

Is Life a Duel ?

Night-Time Sounds in Room 281 - D

The Day She Came to Visit

Memory

Pain

A Pain can be a wound, on hand or foot,
Or more acute than that, Afflict the body and the Soul,
A pain can be a hurt to pride, or feelings
Which are bruised.

A pain can be the perpetrator, who causes such a deed
That soul and feelings are affected, by words so aptly tossed
At hope and longing by your heart, for something not foreseen.
This pain has done some harm to you, to fend a contact between us both,
With qualms and life's precarious whim.

A pain was I, to play with you,
And play with your emotion.
What worth am I, who cannot see,
Some feelings have developed,
From this brief contact,
In such, short space in time?

Why hide from such an opportunity,
To learn and share some conversation with this soul
Of new acquaintance just established?

Why is it that, aloof I stay, for fear of showing fondness?
Thus causing pain, and heart did spurn.
Was it dread, of a possible rejection?
So pain I feel, for having caused this hurt, this ache
To friendship hardly nurtured.

A greater pain I feel for this, a show of coward's folly
To lead you to anticipation, when afraid I am, to follow through
To meet halfway and set things right,

What are the pains? Emotions, which are stirred,
Then tossed aside, so blindly by this fickle person.
He causes pain to others as well as self-inflicted.

February 18, 2001

The Ravages of Time

Look into this mirror, and see the lines of time.
Look at the old photos, and behold another form.
I look, I see a young man, but when I blink, I've aged,
I see some creases of the life I've led.

I look upon this body and see what it can do,
But I ache when I have done too much,
And notice wrinkles on my brow,
From worrying too much.

I look upon a young lass, and no longer feel the stirrings
In loins, which have aged along with this soul.
I only wish I were young again,
To do what I could have done, so many moons ago.

The ravages of time have left my eyes with weakness,
Or arms that are too short. So now I carry on my nose,
Corrective measures so my sight can admire those much
 younger,
Who will one day be likewise inclined, to see what time can bring.

I carry around a pillbox, which the doctor says I need,
By popping little helpers, for my pump to keep at speed.
It must be the life I've led, my heart complains at times
So taking little capsules will give me more time they say.

I wish that I, not spent by time,
Could remain as young as once,
Then like all others I must share that road,
And go as others have done before.

Are we ravaged, or do we look at time gone by,
And wish forever would be now?
Or, are we like the land that's parched,
From life . . . that has gone by?

January 16, 2003

How Do I Speak?

I wrote to you. Or did I?
I said to you. Did I?
Or wish I'd said! Perhaps that is why you did not hear me,
Perhaps that's why you did not hear my plea.

I'd beckoned to you yesterday, but you were not here to see me,
I'd called your name, but silence only replied. With a sigh of wind,
A chilling feeling swept over me, as I feared you'd never know I
needed you,
Or would I see you once again, this day, this week or ever once
again?

Did I call you, the other day, or thought so? I would not say
If, I was by your side today, and talk to you this way.
What would we say if only once we had met?
Would we look into those distant eyes, so deep set?

Was it you, who needed me for comfort and care?
Did you just wish you had taken that dare
To call me, and see if we'd chance to meet,
Or maybe go and have a real treat ?

Did we speak with words, or with silence?
Making it hard to understand, what we are trying to show
or express in our heart,
If we verbalize not, the thoughts which abound,
When sight of each other makes chase in our veins.

I must learn to speak with words and with jest,
So you may understand all the rest.

July 24, 2004

Anger -- At Me or Because of Me ?

She looked at me
With scorn and marked lines upon her brow
Her eyes did sear
When my reply was to dance, but not now.

Pain I did see in her clouded face
And words I heard in short timely space,
The dance steps we've not mastered yet
As my legs, will not keep the pace that's set.

There are some paces and pirouettes
Which neither one will to memory set,
And then my concentration be distracted yet
When I see others there, of my distant past.

Yes dance we do and at times enjoy
But, dance is her rejoice and passion.
Yes, dance I enjoy to music great,
But I do not make an obsession.

What will become of this pastime,
Which we share, with others also?
Will this anger dictate that I leave
And she continues with some other?

To dance is to rejoice in partnership,
In tempo and step to the music, and in sync with each other.
Shall anger reign the time we have
Or do we say that it is all not worth the bother?

Shall we dance, with smile and
Leave anger behind
Or just be
Concerned with anger?

November 7, 2004

Which is my Strength?

I am not solid like the Oak
  Perhaps much more, like the Willow.
I am a man of feelings, just the same as any other.
  Yet how I perceive the things I See, and Hear
  Will determine how I will deal with them,
  And then relate to others who are near.

What do I see ? Or How do I see ?
  Is it with open mind and feeling ?
  Or do I block out all perception, with things
  I have trouble in dealing?

What am I ? Or what should I be,
  In the eyes of others who search the Oak ?
  I am of strength, but like the willow, my feelings tender be.
  Not like the oak, which carries the weight
  Yet never feels emotion
  Of what my heart and soul do see.

How would I rather be?
  I cannot change what the Lord had granted me.

Monday, November 8, 2004

The Little Vampire

Last night I had a visitor
 While finally sound asleep.
She gently grasped my arm and shook
 The cobwebs, from my slumber.

She softly stroked my arm and smiled
 As she whispered in my ear
" I've come to draw some blood from you "
And in the dim light, a glint I beheld
Alight upon her beautiful eyes.

She came around to my other arm
 Deftly working, with precision skill.
And before I realized she was done,
 ' Four Vials ' of my life had spilled.

To compensate for my sacrifice,
 She injected a Saline broth.
Then left with a smile, and parting words
 " When you least expect, we'll be back again
for just a little more."

Sunday, February 6, 2005

When will it end, this life of mine? When will this duel be over?

Is life a duel?

OH yes

Between the will to go on and the will to let it all go

And hover in the balance,

on the pinnacle of the triumph, or the cliff, close to the Abyss

all on the very edge; of life . . . of will, and despair, and also Hope.

There is not much difference between success or failure, just the point at which we are at the maximum of our stress;

stress of elation or dejection.

Does health play a part ? Or the wound in our heart, in our assignment of our place in the game

of life? Oh yes; but more so, the joy in sharing our triumphs and also our load of troubles.

So it will not end, yet ! This life. I must surmount many more pinnacles of challenge;

and of course, their corresponding slide into valleys of despondent fear, only to pick myself up,

and Crawl along, to get back on this ridge of ever greater thrills.

Thrills of living amongst my trials and triumphs,

and sharing these with friends.

So; Yes, this life must go on, our duty it is to take that road, with its many twists and turns and

reversals, but the things we see along the way, the gifts of nature and our friends, make the trek

a joy and blessing. It is a long road, so we must keep a healthy mind, as the destination

will become more meaningful when the road has had its rewards along the way.

The road may be strewn with sunshine and with rain, so we must tread softly, and make great stride.

It is life, this stride, this road we travel. Let us travel it well.

This Duel will be over when the Lord has led us to the door,

at the end of the ribbon we have been following.

So let me choose to be healthy and strong, for the long road to follow.

If I choose right; this life will be long, if permission I've attained from above.

Let me choose the right path, and share it with friends.

And perhaps it will not end so soon, as the road I have chosen has yet much for me to see.

Tuesday, February 22, 2005

Night-Time Sounds in Room 281 - D

The beds they creak, while some do Slumber
And then some shift as their occupants Rumble.
One coughs, while the other Wheezes,
Out in the hallway, someone Sneezes

The staff looks in from time to time,
At their desks a few had managed to dine.
Last night there was some loud Commotion,
The Lady across, should have required a Sleeping Potion.

The Man across my side, got a Transfer
To get away from this constant Ramble,
Which lasted almost all night,
From this Lady in great Mental Plight!

I Wonder if she, here should be ? Or
Moved to the ' Douglas ' before we all ask to leave.

Sunday, February 6, 2005.

My stay at the Cardiac Unit, JGH Montreal.

The Day She Came to Visit

It was a dreary day out
with a heavy, dark cover of clouds.
They seemed to hang just above rooftops,
and disburse some flakes of snow.

The Staff had transferred her to this floor
from the operating room below.
Her fall was not the average one,
as her aged bones are frail
and thus her hip she fractured.

All her family came to visit in a group
and after a while, there remained just one.
She sat there silently, while her Nan was sleeping;
Holding an afternoon vigil, she for her Grandma.

This young lady who has been fondly attached
to her Nan, since she was very young,
Now turns the tide of time, and instead
The young one sits by her side.

November 2, 2004

Written for lady in next bed over from my Mom.

Memory

What is it that you said? I seem to have misplaced
This train-of- thought, of what you called your name.
Why is it that I cannot recall,
The events of Yesterday, when all of Yesteryear
Is clear as if it happened just today?

What is it that I said? Is it the second Time,
Or more often, this tale I've told to you,
On this day and those before? Again I've forgotten what
I've said, and even misplaced your name.

Please help me try to understand,
Why all these thoughts are scattered in my brain,
Disconnected from the flow of events, and time.
I've lost it, or just misplaced again, in my haste
To assemble, in proper order, this train of thought,
Of recollection, of where I went, and what I did, of late
And even minutes just elapsed.

So many years ago it had transpired, this
Glorious experience. I see it now so clear, in detail
Like a tapestry, as if I was there now, re-living.
But what I said, or where I've been, or who
Was with me yesterday, has passed into oblivion.

I fear this Loss, of names and thoughts,
Events, and even places, where I was,
I even forget of where I have to go.
Please help me find these wayward thoughts,
And unite the recollections of those bygone days,
With those, which now just past.

Is it my age, or just the life I've led
Which prevents the flow of thoughts, and places
From being clear in mind?
*   Why can I, not Remember?*

January 29, 2002

Chapter 8: Nourishment of Body and Soul

Friends in Music

My Glass of Wine

Musik Governs My Day

A Pause, Tea Break or Coffee if you Please

A Thought When Cutting Onions or
    Other Slippery Things

Grappa

Voice

Music … and Song Are a Voice in the Night

Cream Cheese with Bacon

Waffles and Waffles

The Sandman

Rain

Friends in Music

A friend of music is a person
Who wishes to listen in rapture and joy,
To Melody and Symphony
Of ideas and sounds, Composers had put on score.

This friend is here as
Audience, which the Musician needs,
For Composer's masterpiece to celebrate
And listen with enchantment and meditation.

This friend, Performer and Composer is that
Artist whom we call upon,
When our inner selves seek solace;
And Harmony will pry us from our shell.

These friends are Audience
Who share their ecstasy with
Others who have need to express
And draw from Musicians their deepest feeling.

This enraptured audience
Share their happiness and elation, with
Others as profoundly smitten,
By thunderous applause for this rendition.

This Friend is that person
Who has come to need,
This voice in music to express his pain
And share the inner sorrows, which engulf him.

Musicians and Friends will reminisce the Spontaneity,
The Exuberance, and Adventure
Of having partaken and shared this
Musical Experience.

March 22, 1997

My Glass of Wine

I choose this Goblet as a Vessel
  To hold my precious drink,
While entertaining guests at home
Who've come to taste of my Wine Collection.

.

This Vessel has great depth
  When filled again, to brimming rim.
Now as we sample some vintage from other years
  The conversation does get slurred of sorts.

.

At some point, out come titbits
  Of bread and spread and cheese bits.
With names that sound like 'Hors D'Oeuvres'
  To try to abate the effects of les 'Oeuvres du Vin. '

Back to this depth of Goblet, it is not all so deep
  But now the conversation is of such
That one would almost fall asleep.
  Oh yes! The depth, t'was only the run of words
As subjects lost importance, but intent became profound
  When all of us, became more vocal, and tried to utter a sound.

Next day some glasses with wine were deep,
  Which some did not finish, as they had fallen asleep.
And now we all nourish a well-deserved pain
  in our head, as we really got drunk again.

Next time I should choose a smaller goblet,
    when I sample a selection of my wine.

Tuesday, November 9, 2004

Musik Governs My Day

At the End of the Day, Will you Sing for Me?

I sometimes wish to sing a song,
And hope that you will sing along.
If I could only hold a tune,
I'd feel like being on the moon.

Your voice has such a silvery sound,
That one would think you're Opera bound.
Every other day you sing for me
Well before breakfast, while sipping tea.

To get your morning voice in tune
I play along from the piano stool.
Together we play in Harmony,
Rather than listen to a symphony.

Once breakfast has ended we both take our leave
For town, through traffic snarls, we will weave.
But all day long, at work I pray,
That at day's end, again we'll play.

By and by, after many a year, your perseverance brings reward,
When the Dean of the Academy presents your Music Award.
You have earned your degree, as attested by this official scroll,
A Masters in Musik; Voice, as your instrument of Choice.

We know not what the future will bring,
As you travel the world at concerts to sing.
You've mastered the works of Composers Great,
Yet still, you sing for me in the evening late.

I wish that I could sing with you,
But then all who listen, their face would turn blue.   .
So all I do is hum along
As you so artfully sing my song.

Sunday, November 14, 2004

A Pause, Tea Break or Coffee if you Please

A rest, and time to relax
>   Unwind the Muscles, Body and Mind.
A time to plan the day ahead,
>   And reminisce of what transpired,
Up to this present time.

A Time to stretch the arms and back,
>   Reduce the tension found,
From sitting at your desk too long,
>   At keyboard, while computer bound.

You plan your day, the evening that is to come.
>   What will you eat tonight?
Or will you call your loved ones,
>   To surprise them with an invitation
To go out, feast, and see some sight.

Just then you realize,
>   The short time you've just spent in Reverie,
Is over once again.

September 8, 2000

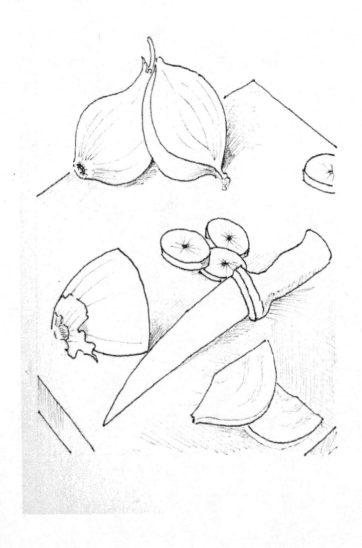

A Thought When Cutting Onions, or Other Slippery Things

Watch the fingers today
  they are very valuable they say,
  and as the day progresses
  you need them for the fond caresses.

So be kind to those DIGITS, as they are kind enough to you,
  they stroke you when you are blue .
  They make you sparkle in the shower,
  and help you every hour. So be kind to those members of your hand,
  and life will then, not be so bland.

With work, they wile away the hours,
  so you will then receive the dollars
  to spend on frivolous items,
  with which you will play, in your hand,
  if it not protected by a dressing band.

SO!   BE KIND TODAY FOR YOUR SAKE
  And watch when you cut that steak ...

    BE KIND

                    Tuesday, September 14, 2004

Grappa

The name, it comes from the Grape
  And the Italians love to sample this drink
  It's made from the fruit of the Vine.
  And when the Vintner presses his grapes
  He takes pity on the goods that remain
  So he sweetens them and sets to Ferment.
  Then after a few months his patience is spent,
  As he waits for this product, but not until Lent.

So this Vintner does ply his secret trade,
  A Magician he becomes as he
  Transforms this Brew of his labour of Love
  Into concoction, of a delightful brew
  Since it comes from the grape, it is NOT named a stew.

The French they call it " Cognac "
  If, only from that Provence it's made.
  As other sources are not permitted
  To Affiché, as per rules of the State,
  for the name is reserved for that Provence by the Committée.

This Committée is governed by people of influence and political ties
  To prevent others of going along for a ride
  On the backs of the founders of the 'Provence de Cognac'
  In brewing their own of quality great.
  Thus they end up with little choice, in appellation they search for a Dandy
  And end up with a name like "Brandy"

The German-speaking peoples, they call this drink " Weinbrandt "
  It matters not, what source of the grape
  as long as it's really sweet, so they can make
  more, of this lovely treat, and get flustered from the induced heat
  when they set the remnants of this Wine into ' Brandt '

Be it Cognac, Grappa or Winebrandt, it will leave you sighing
  with pleasure
  As in your hand, another glass, you treasure.

Will you hold it, toast with it, or send it down the hatch?
  It surely is another great batch.

Thursday, November 11, 2004

Voice

This morning I heard a heavenly voice,
While Mass I did attend,
From Loft above, it rang through Church
Like a song direct from Heaven,

It sang so clear that all did wonder,
Of where, this call came from.
It made me think of this Gift
Which God provides, to all his Children dear.

Only few of them can sing so clear,
This is a heavenly talent
Which lifts the hearts of all who hear
This instrument created for us by God.

She sings the Hymns, while leading the choir
And lifts the voice of all; in song and praise of
Church and Lord and people all around.
Meek am I to hear such clear and velvet tone.

This singer, ' Pat ' has lifted up my soul,
With music and voice so clear,
It made me think of all of us,
Who love to sing so fine. If only we had a voice to
complement her skill,
When we all sing along, and not be out of line.

This voice is music of the of highest order,
Produced by chords which were not created by man,
But given to us by our Creator himself,
When he made, Woman and Man.

This voice is great in Solo and Group,
And Choir of mixed Girls and Boys,
As she leads us through Prayer and Hymns to our Lord,
With her gift of Music, through Song.

Sunday, October 29, 2000

Music . . . and Song,
Are a Voice in the Night

As I talk away the night with you,
I sit in amazement and awe, it's true,
Maybe it's your charm or passion I see,
It could be your honesty and frankness with me,
We laugh and we talk as we enjoy the night,
Hours keep passing until it is light,
I'm having a feeling I can't quite explain,
Like the comfort you feel in a mid-summer's rain...

The lines you are writing have a voice of their own
and I see you are sometimes so terribly alone
Be it calm or a selection of words which I chose
As words are a passion in everyone's prose
I select them with reason, to delight readers' senses
To give them some reason to verify all those tenses.
What passion do you envision, in these short words with me
You can explain them while sipping a big mug of Tea
Share that with banter and a giggle or two
and we'll get some Cantor to sing a line just for you.
Before I end this, I give credit to you for courage to seek,
with a smile to some stranger, who is as far as a walk by a creek.

August 8, 2003

Cream Cheese with Bacon

Cream Cheese with Bacon
  on Bagel she wished.
 Which sounds quite different
    From, Dietician's preferred dietary list.

She said it is delicious
  That I try some, some time.
Well my Cardiologist prefers
  I not step out of line.

Now the Bagel & Cream Cheese
  Give nourishment – light,
But the Bacon would give my
  Arteries some Blockage & Plight.

September 9, 2005

Waffles and Waffles

Waffles and Waffles they have ridges and bumps,
Turn them over and there are corresponding lumps.
Fill them with cherries and berries and other things too,
for a snack in the evening between us two.

Make them in irons and make them galore,
When you need snacks you pop them in Toaster.
Spread on the Honey, Cherries or Berries when they pop
out so soon. Forget not the filling or whipping cream too,
Then pop them by mouthfuls and savour the flavour right through.

They have ridges . . . and dimples and hollows for filling,
as we wait, around the iron we're milling
Like puppies awaiting a treat.
They come out so hot, that our fingers will burn from the heat.

Heavenly soft they become when lathered with cream,
and all those berries and cherries and likes.
Savour the flavour of a delight while we eat quite a few,
As we play in our loving, of delights just with you.

December 11, 2005

The Sandman

Let the sandman visit you lightly
By a waning moon, and fill your vision
With dreams of a morning so soon,
That you remember them, till well after noon.

It was long ago Mother had told us
This interesting tale, when fear of sleep
Fought a battle, its battle in the gloom
Under covers . . . in the dark room.

So She sat by our side and read a tale
Or maybe two, till the Sandman sprinkled grains in our eyes,
Then we rubbed them to shut out the light,
Of candle and lamp light, and sighs filled the room.

Still She sat by our sides, to keep fear of the parting
Then cover our sides, and sing a Lullaby
And sooth our great fears,
As she wipes away our tears from the avenged fears.

Sandman protect us, and let our sleep come,
For morning will shortly be here.
Then grains we will rub from our eyes,
As proof you were here.

October 7, 2002

Rain

It falls from above, where dark clouds loom
and dance in the sky to cast a sombre gloom
upon all who have want of sunshine
and the warmth which is surely to come.

Our farmers pray for it, these nourishing droplets
until enough has been spilled, and creeks overfill.
Then they pray that it stops or else the crops will be spoiled,
and the flooding will wash away the precious soil.

Like a Pall, the dark clouds hang over the city
hiding rays, that warmth should bring,
laden with droplets, that threaten to fall
and shower the greenery and birds and us all.

It replenishes lakes by the rivers it fills
that collect all the surplus which run down the hills.
It seeps into crevises and fissures for land's thirst to quell.
and for farmers who pray for it, it replenishes their well.

After many a day, of these downpours and showers
we've all had enough, it's drowning the flowers,
and dampens our spirits, so we pray to the Lord,
to turn off the spiggot and send down instead, if we use the right word,
some warm rays of the Sun,
so the children can go out and have fun.

We just got over Winter, and we desperately crave
Sun; to usher in Summer, so we can bathe.
And bask in its warming embrace
And renew health before next winter's advancing race

December 10, 2005

Chapter 9: Retirement

Retirement

Quarter Century Club Party

When I Retired I Had a Wish

Retirement

My retirement is when I can say,
"To hell with getting up this morn."
No haste to chase the Convoys,
On roads, with ribbon of traffic.

A waste it is to rush, then find
My desk piled high with stacks of things,
So now I look and sympathize,
With the soul who will replace me.

Now is the time to get to know our loved ones,
As we were never home,
And when we were, the phone would ring,
Then out we'd run, for some emergency,

Which requests our presence be at work,
If only to help get coffee made, for the crew
Who worked so hard to set things right,
Needing only moral support,
And answer that 'ringing thing.'

I'll dream of you all, when fish are biting,
Wish all of you could come and join.
Then why would I invite you all?
No Routine, I do follow.

Now just the time, when construction comes to peak,
I pack my guns, and Moose to seek,
A sortie with my friends likewise inclined,
Traipse through the brush,

To follow a trail or spur,
We're sure we saw just down the way,
Of large Bull which we dreamt about,
While work was still our day.

I got this one, and what a rack,
He sports on head so great.
We clean the meat and truck it home,
Perhaps a second one we find,
Before we leave the hunting blind.

We may just get the Better Half to come along,
Next time.
While ducks we search with Faithful friend,
Four-legged friend it be.

To send him out to fetch,
The game, which Providence permitted us that day.
We give him a pat and say to the Wife
" That was a great hunting day."

Woe did we trust Her shooting skill,
Which matched our feeble aim,
And bettered us again this time
To prove, she is the Better Half.

At home again, we know the recipes,
For duck and goose and hunted moose,
For meals, invited those who hunt with us,
And our spouse cooked most of it,
While we knew all the spices,
Which add that special flavour.

It was a meal, and reminisce we do,
What would the Guys and Gals at work,
Think of this free time, we've been granted ?
If only they could do the same,
And tell their boss to " . . . it ! "

T'is nice to be at home at daybreak,
The coffee to Her bedside bring,
Not just on Sunday morn.
Then help her in the kitchen,
With chores, we are not certain how they're done,
For we were never home.

There is no Boss from Work to show us how,
And coach us when we're slow.
Yes shy we are to learn so late,
From the New Boss now at home.

We strive to get the order right,
And find the warehouse pantry, under sink
For storage of the pots and pans,
Which we must place just right.

Now come to cleaning toilets
And making beds at morn,
We cannot tell the kids to do,
They're gone and we're alone.

Now do I get into Her hair?
With all my fussing over, what I had thought
Should be done this other way.
But now I'm not the Boss any more,
It has to go Her Way.

Does she wish me to be back at work ,
Or want me round her daily?
Or do I leave and golf some more,
And be home just as rarely?
Maybe take her with me shopping,
And share My likes with her,
Or Hers with me.

We look back at the time we worked,
Now, at the home we need adjusting
To a New life-style we accept,
When joining those Retired.

When will I be forgotten, by friends and colleagues
Who've meant so much to me? Or will I be remembered
for the
Opportunity I've given them to learn,
To fill my shoes, when I have done,
What I'm doing here this day ?

Retiring.

September 19, 1998

Quarter Century Club Party

Twenty five years, of work and of strain
Is a quarter century, of friends and of gain?
Now what you are seeing, it rings with a pain,
To watch them all leaving, to seek a new life.
Retired and travelling, to rekindle their fire of life.

A party is set for this milestone achieved
Where we just gather and ponder the past.
The fact we had made it, we all are relieved
As we wait for those newcomers coming up in the ranks.
Managers are delighted, when old timers come,
To hear all the new things, and recall tales that will last.

Two bits of years and two bits of lore
Might sound like sailors, just back from the shore.
Twenty-five years of those memories cast
How we forget them, if only we last.
Then comes this smart-ass with memory skill,
Of how we had handled the boss's Bar-Bill.

Two bits of words from Director and more
And others will add some to make it a score.
As many as are here, more two-bits are told
Then add some more two bits,
And a century of history we are to behold.

That we had succeeded, so well and so long
Is the reason, why we feel oh so strong.
We come to this party, to chat and reminisce
Of all the activities, which went nearly amiss,
Brought loved ones along, so they can share with our past
And hope that this party forever will last.

October 6, 2000

When I Retired I Had a Wish

For all the years I'd worked at this place,
I shared some wit and took up space.
I worked alone most of the time, because my boss
Just never had time to check on me, or see me do,
What I was paid to say I did.

All of these bosses who now are gone,
And those who've replaced them will not come,
Now it's too late, as I am gone.

Some pride I had, while contacts made,
And worked alone out in the field,
While supervising digs, and tile-drained fields,
Or ditches cleaned in rain and sleet,
So we could please our customers, and have their work complete,
And our Pipeline was protected.

If only once someone came along to say or see what we had done,
But time would not permit them from their shelter stray.

Now I'm gone; The day I left, not a soul of the bosses said word, nor note,
Nor " thank you " for our offering, of twenty-plus years of life and time,
To this, a Changing Company.
The Company changed, and so did Value, of what we offered of life and soul,
Not even Manager, nor man above, could utter a thank-you for the time we shared.
Is this a trend of change?
T'is sad to see such added value. Is this not the motto of our statement?
Added value, but what value was there for our effort,
In making this company, once so great?

Shamed am I to see such loss, what Richard Walker valued,
And some of his followers also respected in their management ways,
To recognize an employee for what he had contributed,
But now it's Lost, as we heard not a word, as we Three, departed.

Can this a great company be, when respect is lost,
For some of the men who helped build it to greatness ?
Or was it one time, when we had people, who cared
For the work and the value we offered.

This saddens me so, along with my colleagues,
Who have also been offered this package.
Can we, now at this time, see what value this company has come to ?
Should we care, if they cared not for us, or just leave with our pride,
As there was no-one to bid us farewell, from the team above?
We've worked as a team, for a company once great,
And left on this day, a future to see,
And not a message we heard from above.
We were great long ago, and proud to be known.

We worked for them once,
Was it great? The world yes, but this company ?
Yes we did our share, to add value to shares,
 But no one, to share our departure.

We were proud; but now

We have parted.

My Wish did **not** come true.

Chapter 10: Leisure and Sports

Dream of the Water

Dance

Bonnie

Learning to Dance

A Paddle

Fly Fishing

The Campfire Meal

My Old Cycle

A Whale, She did See on the Sea

My Brother's Old Cycle

Why do I Wait ?

Dream of the Water

When you take a drop,
Think of the water when you search for sanity to keep. Swim in it,
paddle over it or lie back and relax beside it.
Fishermen do it for sport and for leisure, with rod or a cane,
and it is always in water they strive to be sane.

Wash with it, or mix it in paints, and then paint it to scene
depicting the feelings from inspiration you gain.
Sail on it or dive in it, or swim through it for sport,
or do it as others who have rehabilitations of sort.

Mix it with drinks of some whisky and wine, and then sit down
with lover or friends when you dine.
Add some tea bags or beans of the coffee to flavour again,
and drink more of the
Life-giving fluid for a refrain.

Now when you sleep, don't dream of it or else you'll feel wet,
and be inclined to blame it on the household pet.

Live with it or play in it but use it with care,
As a clean source, is becoming so awfully rare.

Yes, Agua, Aqua, Water or Wasser or whatever name
you wish to share,
Enjoy it ! . . . As it is sent down from the heavens with flair.

July 24, 2004

Dance

A ritual it is amongst the Animal Kingdom
To prance about alone or in a group
And try to impress one another,
Especially, the other gender.

In Birds it is a courtship display
As the pair will each attempt to impress one another.
Or perhaps take flight and perform aerial stunts
To try to win the other.

Some carnivores prance all about and try to sniff.
With some males it is a show of strength as they
Challenge to battle another encroaching suitor,
While they walk about, rigid and stiff.
The length of his mane and prowess of his Hunting skill
Is rewarded by a mate, for having brought in a kill.

The Herbivores large, some sport antlers so great
With deep colour of mane and stature quite large,
As they prance and then dance before suitable partner,
And then try to coax them to become their new mate.

The smaller creatures have similar traits
When they scamper and scurry
As HE brings the material
Which for Bedding will be,
As they both dance about in a glee.

Now, mankind will dance or be silent and still
As not everyone has the rhythm and skill
And most fellows would rather chat and gather
On sidelines with drink in their hand
And then ogle the ladies and young girls who dance
With great grace and such skill.

Then there are some of us,
Ladies and Men, who wish to learn more than to prance about
With lack-less skill,
So we sign up for courses to learn
The Rumba, and Samba and more steps to name
That will become sessions in learning, much more than a game.

Once mastered, which may take yet many a Year
These partners will receive compliments, coming to Ear
Every once in a while, a Banquet or Ball will not bring a fear
As they learned them all and their fear of skill, will not bring a tear.
Cha-Chas and Tangos and Meringue to boot
They even dance Mambo and Waltz with a hoot.

Now Quick-Step and numerous more
I cannot count them, as they are more than a score.

Now do we impress our partner or date,
or just the others who are trying to learn, oh so late?
We can also try to dance as a pre-amble to sex
Only now we will not read from a text.

Let us dance and impress our partners
And those all around, with all we had learned
From our teacher, as her eyes stare us down,
Again we just feel like were burned.

Shall we Dance ?   . . . .

Thursday, November 11, 2004

Bonnie

Bonnie said Practice,
And Practice we do
Every time we lace up our delicate shoes.

We do it alone, and we do it in pairs
We try to do it without her seeing our fears
We turn and we twist, in a step and a whirl
And still she looks down at our feet in a scorn.

Then we do it to music and we do it again
Still the steps are too cumbersome, and the mind is not set,
To follow the rhythm and the beat of the song,
And thus we are not keeping our steps right along.

In miniscule details she has been trying
To teach us just right, now and before,
As we come from aft and a bit just before
Were supposed to, in pace and in step
With the details she'd just shown.

When we watch her perform, as she did the other Saturday night,
We realize all her attention
To the details in step and in stride,
Make our effort seem fruitless and hopefully far,
In striving to reach such perfection and look of approval
From our Bonnie thus far.

Many thanks for the effort and patience you give to teach us your skill.

May 10, 2004

Learning to Dance

Guilt has beset me, this morning so Fair
For we did not dance, but played in our Lair.
For this deed some penance we must pay,
On Dance Floor our feet will not stray.

We try it, and try it, and once more again,
But the movements are cumbersome as we
Repeat them again.

Then to our joyful relief
Bonnie shows us, as we stand there in great disbelief,
All our little gaffs in feet and in stance,
So we watch with a shy little glance.

Now off to lessons, then practice to follow
We'll learn them eventually, then in our glory we'll wallow.

Did you really want to dance with me ?
Or would you rather hide behind the tree,
As we gather in garden, and on fresh mown lawn,
At gathering of friends and dancers alike
With music playing, we'll dance until Dawn ?

Monday, December 6, 2004

A Paddle

It is a work of art, we use to guide
Our solitary craft, through
Silent narrow channels,
And drift us through our reveries.

It moves us over the Silvery
Shining pond, where only the loon
Will call to us, to thrill us
With its haunting sound.

It helps us glide through mists
Of morning dew, and thoughts;
To let us wander in our trail
And forget what is left behind.

Its shape is solid, reassuring,
While the fluid water under bow,
Lifts us gently, in time with
The gentle waves below.

A paddle gives us Power
To surge ahead and rise
Above the crests, and conquer,
Then glide the valley just beyond.

This paddle is a part of us,
Responding to our pulse.
To move ahead, then fall behind,
Exhilarating as we reach towards

Our destination, yet afar,
And settle into cadence, and thrill
Of each successive stroke,
Our campsite thus approaching.

This paddle is our escape
From things which can oppress us,
To help us get away from all,
Only to renew our soul.

August 31, 1995

Fly Fishing

Flies and Flies, the choice is so abundant
  For which one will bite you, before
  You cast it out on line so fine
  And pray that fish will bite first?

Some of them bite, not fish but you, and swell you do
  Not with pride of catch, but pain of flesh taken from your hide.
  Cast fly with rod and it goes lost, when whipped overhead
  Into grass so fine, or hangs up in the branches.

Now take this angler who catches not flies,
  He makes his own to imitate their likes, from feather and thread,
  To look like flies which we could not see,
  As they hide under rock and in the lee,
  With this he casts to a hope and a swirl and if he is lucky
  A trout will burst out of water and whirl.

Sometimes a meal will be made from this catch,
  Or it is released for another to try his good luck,
  Or if you were lucky it will adorn your wall
  To show how a cast of finesse has rewarded you this fine prize.

How to perfect this cast and not catch your ear,
 And send it out in a breeze to its goal
 A spot in the water you had thought should hold bounty.
 Your eyes were tricked by the sunlight, into hopeful glory,
 You dream of a trout on the line,
 When actually you snagged a leaf in the bushes.
 Cast again and its target is true, but not a nibble to be felt
 on your offering,

You change the fly with another from your vest,
 Which the store had said for this day was the best.
 Try once again, to present it to your dream, and loft it to that spot,
 Which you thought will hold your reward.
 Alas, a tug, then a burst from the surface to a light in your eye.

Fly-Fishing is not luck, but the choice of the fly,
 The flick of the rod, cast to trick the fish into thinking of food.
 It is art in the placement, and presentation to where the food
 should be found.
 Hopefully rewards will be brought to your net, for the table
 Or release back to water, while you only practice your skill.

/ Cont'd >>>

We wander all day, to tease fish and be bitten by flies, and the fishing bug.
Lost from our world of problems and stress,
As we stroll along the creek or serpentine stream
In tune with nature, only looking for swirls in the pools as we dream.
Dressed are we for water in rubber and vest, with hardware dangling from strings and small clips, and a net we do carry to land fish and the brambles.
We trade our city troubles for leisure while we ramble,
Through thicket and clearing by stream towards a bend where we know,
Where this pool will await us.

Come evening we land ourselves back in the car, with rewards of a workout or trophy in Creel, and head for the homestead with recipes just swirling.
We plan to prepare, the feast, which God has granted us that day.
Then get home and prepare the fish, then savour its taste,
This feast for a King with a goblet of wine, we will dine,
Amid dreams, of the next foray to stream.

This angler gives thanks for the bounty of game from the waters,
and the sunshine above, and the chance to go out again, hopefully soon.

Now which fly was it that bit me? Can I tie it to hook?

September 3, 2000

The Campfire Meal

The flicker of the flame was mesmerizing us again
while we sat around the crackling fireside

The flames licked at timber, which we tried to set ablaze
as we sat about in stupor and intoxicated haze,

Into smouldering embers we did gaze, while sitting by the edge
        of the campground lair
after dining like the night before, and finished by the waning light
        on soup and sausage with cobs of corn, and a complimenting
salad to the gourmet fare
we washed down the stir-fry, which was done just right,
with wine and beer and our faces were just glowing bright.

Of chefs we numbered three, with helpers jumping all about the tree,
we snacked on Nuts and Swiss chocolate bars sipping cups of
        Herbal Tea,
as we prepared our delicious feast, someone tossed some treats to the
        little chipmunks,
who carried them all away, to some hole in ground or caverns hidden
        all around.

/ cont'd

The Campfire Meal / cont'd

At some point in our reverie, all decided that sleep made its plea
so we all traipsed our way to our canvas hotels.
For me to fall asleep, I had started counting sheep,
then when sleep had finally come, I was wakened by the constant beep,
Just as daylight was announced by the sunrays shining through
the curtains where they tried to cover the plastic window screen.

Now, as we pack up, preparing to depart
we wonder when the next time we'll start,
for all of us to come together again
chancing for to camp, in the pouring rain.

A meal is always gourmet by the campfire side
Thus we plan another cross border ride.
  BUT WHEN ?????

November 16, 2004

My Old Cycle

I learned to ride an adult frame
When little sister beat me to it and put me to shame.
So I climbed aboard, onto pedals between the bars
and Sis held the seat to keep me from falling and seeing the stars.

Some good neighbours gave my Mom a lady's bike,
now little sister and I had something we liked.
All around the barnyard and through the Hay Field we practiced most time
when we were not in Mother's visual line.

Then on the weekend when Dad came home
after the Sunday noon-time meal,
we coaxed him, and let it be known
that we could cycle, and the story was real.

So out to the shed almost dragging we led
him to witness our newfound skill.
So we got on the bikes and cycled up the hill
there we turned around, and back we sped.
Now all of this is an enormous feat
as none of us could even reach the seat.
The horizon of vision, was not from afar,
it was was just over the handlebar.

We never did get our very own
and we felt like we had grown,
as now we were able to get down the road
yet able to come back with a small load.
From the village we raced back,
for fear is something which we certainly did lack,
This made us feel like we were in heaven
as neither of us had reached the age of Seven.

Then in Nineteen Hundred and Fifty Five
we emigrated, across the Big Pond
And in this big city no cycles we would ride,
as little kids into the traffic might slide
into oncoming cars when out for a ride.

Only a few years later my Dad found a bargain
after many months of coaxing
a used five-speed was delivered to our garden.
With my allowance and paper-route money it had been paid
for Thirty-Five dollars a deal was laid.
Now they let me ride farther than up to Beaver Lake
As my very own money, was really at stake.

~~ ~~ ~~ ~~ ~~ ~~ ~~

After many years and countless thousands of miles on a saddle
of a Ten-Speed racing bike, I now use a paddle.
I'm no longer able to treck the roads of my youth
so I park it in the shed,
Only occasionally on pedals do I tred.

The racing bike is mounted on a stand,
in basement I exercise when the girth of my waist
I now cannot stand, the few extra pounds
which have managed to land.

In the year Two Thousand and One
I volunteered as an aid
In the Veterans' Hospital with veterans ... and elderly folks
who needed help and a cheer,
for this we were willing and always so near.
On occasion they have a raffle and ticket draw
So ten tickets and a wish I did secure.

The benefit to be, one-half of the prize for the winner's share
and the other for the veterans' care.
A few days later the Head Nurse gave me a call,
To let me know I should contact the ticket seller first of all.
This contact I made and learned the good news
that I was the winner, the first prize of that draw.
The item I had won was a new Mountain Bike,
so now, with twenty-seven gears I can make another treck.

Now at more than Fifty-Nine,
the Cardiologist talked to me sternly and straight.
She told me to get with it and exercise more,
now pedal I'll start like many years before.

December 10, 2005

A Whale, She did See on the Sea

Oh what a whale!!!!!!
I then read of her tale.
If only I had been there,
I'd also have seen my share.

With others, she was on the Sanctuary
To take in the delights
And from aboard ship see the sights
Of all things she has heard

About these great gentle creatures,
that have some very distinctive features.
They glide past the boat and send out a plume
of some rather foul smelling fume.

The passage is awsome
And many are starstruck
   . . . and maybe a bit sea sick
but would do it more often
as their hearts had been softened
to the plight of the whale
   . . . whose habitat has really gone stale

From Pollution and Harvest
which is really plundering the oceans for profit
with no care for its chain,
which in turn must sustain
the life for our future, and food for our table.
Many of mankind are not able
to recognize the value of sustained life in our sea.

Yes; she wrote of her experience
of observation, while others captured memories to share
on their cameras and pictures to show they really were there,
on the deck of the Sanctuary, on the ocean with Capitain Steph.

So what did they see?
A Sanctuary of water with mystical Whales to delight them
on this great, great Pacific Sea
they saw from Sanctuary.
A sanctuary for the whale, way out from the bay.
Nor far had they to stray, before all were rewarded by a frolicking
      display
Of Nature and Mankind, in Peace and at Play.

Wednesday, October 19, 2005

My Brother's Old Cycle

When Johnny was just a little guy
our father coaxed him to give it a try
He started out on a bike with three wheels
and around the back yard he did peels.
Now mind you, that he learned it fast
and it was definitely not his last.

Then after a while he would not fall
so he got a little scooter, on which he stood tall.
I must admit his knees got scraped
from many a fall he could not escape.
With growth and courage he outgrew that board
so he pleaded with our parents and to the Lord,
that somehow our parents would see his tears

And with Pity, he'd get a real bike.
This was not so, as the money was scarce
and the lodging was sparse
as much as our parents would like
our own home would be more secure
than renting and listening to others' verbal manure.

Now after a few years, out parents did relent
and went to the hardware store, on a C.C.M. the money was spent.
Now Johnny had his own bike,
it had two wheels and no more a trike.

At Fourteen it was a Ten-Speed of his very own,
for the Kid's bike he really had outgrown.
This he paid for with some allowance and paper-route money
and later he peddled out to meet his sweet honey.

Does he still cycle, or is it hung up in basemet like mine ?
Taking preference to sit down and Dine.
Of course you cannot ride . . .
           after you've had a few glasses of wine.

October 23, 2005

Why do I Wait ?

Why do I wait?
I often wonder.
I sit there . . . still,
Amidst thoughts . . . and ponder.

Occasionally I take a glance
Above the newspaper before me spread.
I'm awakened by chance
When new client, to waiting room is Led.

We engage in idle chatter
While at times the intercom statically clatters,
The tranquility is also broken.
So what does it all matter,

As we are here patiently waiting,
When I'd rather be dating
At some Restaurant Fine,
As we select a really good wine?

I should not get too far ahead
It is only morning, and time has not sped.
So I sit here, deep in thought,
Awaiting Inspriation, which comes definitely Not!

So! From time to time I close my eyes
And then realise, this waiting I do despise.
Soon dreams drift by, and comfort I found
To be shattered so soon by a calling sound

" Your Car is Ready "
So I arise, unsteady
To go and pay my debt.
Looking at my credit card, I would have wept.

So . . . Think not of the idle time
You sit in that waiting room.
It costs just as much as if you stood in line,
To dispense with your money so soon.

Why do we wait to pay so much?
Our cars are our trusty steed,
And to keep it healthy, we give of such,
Our Time, and Money without greed.

December 28, 2005

Chapter 11:   Family

Ann

Dad

The Hospital Visit
    Sequel to a Mild Stroke

Lost on the Geriatric Ward

Ann

She is my Sister, a Special one
And Dear, She cared for me when I was
Younger, and still after many a Year.

She cared for our Brother, and little Sister too,
And still she worries, about us, and comes to our aid,
When we feel down, and in need of some Care.
When we were younger, she bundled us along,
Giving up her own youth, by always carrying us with her.
Like baggage we were, to her chance of being like other
young Girls.

She lifts my Spirit when my focus I do lose,
And guides me through my setback,
A steady course for to choose,
Forgetting her own Woes, as if nothing to lose.

She handles her household with care and delight,
One should be honoured to visit a dwelling so bright.
Her Family is well-fed, and cared for, all right.
Both Children do draw from her wisdom and skill,
To make their own life, and house with such skill.

When Grandchildren come, they only want Her,
It is the care they are searching, which is different;
Because it is " Oma ", and love they do see,
As she loved both Martin and Anne-Marie.

Experience and love are all she has shown,
Hiding her own frailties, and fears, and concerns.
Neglecting her health, to give others her care,
When it is we who should give help to her now,
As she has done for us, through all these years.

Who is she, This great Sister of mine? a Sibling, a Friend,
A Confidante, and Healer, and Mentor of Skills.
She taught me to cook, for patience she had, to show
Why my first tries were never quite bad, only she would sample,
Then tell me just why, it should be done different, at the next try.

She helped me with Homework, with Reading and Math,
Foregoing her own hope in learning more crafts.
She also helped me cope, with Uncertainties of blossoming Youth,
Then tried to explain, why my Hormones affected my change.

Is she Special ? For me, much more so!
She is my Inspiration, when I feel low,
My strength, for all that she can do.
She is my bright light, for knowledge I draw
From her wisdom of things, I'm sure to attain.

I treasure the Wool Sweater, she made for me
Many a decade ago, 35 years it will be shortly.
She made it with love, and care for her Brother,
To last all these years, so I wear it with Pride,
As a token to the love and care she provides.

I try to help her, and feel of her pain,
Even when I have not seen her in days that have passed,
I can see she hides worries and fears, But I feel them,
As if they were mine, because the feeling is strong,
Between Brother and Sister, as special as She.

On this remarkable Day, a Day to remember your Birthday,
These years you have spared, to care for us all
And Family to add, We all wish you a very Special Day.

A Very Happy Birthday,

    From your Brothers and all of your family.
    And all the attached ones, and Little ones too.
    These are only a few of all the voices
    Who wish you the best.

                                        March 15, 2000

Dad

My father was my means of transport,
From Cradle, to Carriage, and then the almighty Wheelbarrow.
He would get me around, along with all of us children.
As older I became, he taught me to ride a Bicycle, not one of kiddie size,
But adult size where between the bars I would stand askance,
And ride the barnyard trail.

He taught me how to heft an Axe, and work with hammer and saw,
But did I want to hear his tale, of how to do it safely?
It just went in one, then out the other ear,
For listen we could not.
As habit was, he said it often, and once was enough for us.

The thrashing I received from time to time, kept me on straight and narrow,
And taught me Honour of my word, which now is my daily motto.
I learned a lot, and to this day, I have not listened to all I have to learn,
As time slips slowly by, I may not have the time to spend
With him, as years glide by, but I do see how the Great Grandchildren,
Are learning from him now.

Where have the years gone, since I was a child, the times we spent at play,
and learn from Dad, all that he taught, to use till present day? May the
Lord let me learn yet this day, for Dad has more to teach the wisdom he
has gained.
And may the Lord maintain his Health, so he will teach us all tomorrow.

Thank You, Dad for all I have learned.

June 18, 2000

The Hospital Visit
Sequel to a Mild Stroke

We come again to visit Mom,
Annie, Dad, Trudi and I.
Mom, she came here almost two weeks ago
Whence from bed at night she fell.

The doctors said there was no damage
All scans were done again
She'd had some bout with Vertigo and perhaps this managed
To cause her sudden fall.

The Doctors made her pass some tests
And many more were done
Now all we know is what we've found
Her memory of short-term things . . .
Is all distorted now.

At times we ask a thing or two
And answers she does give,
But on occasion they are such
they have no bearing on the things
of which she had been asked.

What Ails her ? Or what goes on within her mind ?
I had thought, perhaps she had a Mini-stroke
Which caused her sudden fall
Or is it something more than that
To erase short memory, first of all?

What can we hope for?
Is there a simple cure?
In light of all the research done
The specialists . . . Are not really sure.

Now as a family, we must close our ranks
And to the Lord we must give thanks.
As this episode of mother's life,
More serious could have been,

To create her inner strife.
It was a mini-stroke after all,
So deal with it, we must.
As the age can possibly bring much more,
So pray we will, that the Lord will give
Many, many more years for her to live.

November 22, 2004

Lost on the Geriatric Ward

My God! What has happened to her?
Fear is clearly visible in her eyes,
it was only two weeks ago we brought her in
by ambulance, to get her cared for.

Again she fell beside the bed at night
when disoriented she became.
The later tests confirmed our thoughts,
as her speech, was all disjoined.

Our questions to her received a reply,
the answer was on another subject
not related to the things enquired,
so it seems her thoughts are mired

In other parts of the brain which cannot recall
the events of now, Yet all the past is focused.
More tests by various specialists and none has offered
a reply to concerns which we try to verse.
One thing is for certain, a stroke she had was sure.

Social workers and the medical staff
are treating her in rehabilitation,
speech is coming back so slow,
now all she feels is great frustration
of being lost on the ward.

" When can I come home? " she exclaims
" When can I do my things? "
She cannot go down stairs any more
without someone beside her.
        When will she go Home ?? . . . !!

November 19, 2004

Chapter 12: The Word

A Word

A Light Shone from the Other Side

Poetry Reading at the Yellow Door Coffee House

A Dreamer or a Poet

To Wait

Crippled

Lion Seminar / Laian Seminar

New Year 2006

A Word

Word, it has four letters.
It is a combination of characters, of Vowels and of Nouns.
Place them in an order, and thoughts then resound.
Now choose the right ones, in a sequence, and be eloquent too
Forming a sentence, phrase or a tale, just from you.

Some words, to verse a tender thought, are hard to put to sounds
As words are never clear enough, for feelings in your heart.
If only you could learn some more, to put to lovely tune,
Then sing them like the Lark, it would be heavenly trill,
And please this captive ear, on hearing such a skill.

Speak with me, say to me, and see if I listen still,
To those rambling tirades, tales of enchanting delight,
Which bring me such laughter, or tears of respite.
Chide me for feigning, attentive concern,
When tale is of misfortune, or unfathomable lore.

Speak to me, say to me, with eyes and a smile
Then maybe the language or thoughts will beguile.
Sing to me, with silvery voice in delight,
Like a lark in the morning, when up at first light,
I will listen, to the sound of your voice,
Such is this music, my music of choice.

Share with me sorrows, share with me mirth,
I hear them from adults and children at birth.
Share with me songs, for it is music of life,
Share with me feelings of longing and strife.
Share with me love, and the song will be great.
Dance with the words that the heavens create.

October 3, 2000

A Word

Ein Wort

un Mot

A Light shone from the other side,

A Candle flicker sent its warmth

To set the mood, and light provide

For Diners, just departed.

When you snuffed out its

Amber shimmer, it no longer

Shone my way. Then when you smiled

As you went by, it Brightened up my Day.

Extinguish not a light,

Which illuminates your way.

September 9, 2000
Donauschwaben Club, Scarborough, Ont.

Poetry Reading at the Yellow Door Coffee House

We come to give a listen
  To visions of others' dreams
We lend an ear to others' tales
  And learn a thing or two
Of how we should recite our verse
  When we are in their shoes.

We strain our ears and tune our minds
  To try to fathom what is said
By voice so silent and almost still,
  So we look close and crane our necks to hear the silent trill.
  We adjust our hearing
  When next reader booms his voice,
In tirade of a thought so clear
  It just boggles our minds as we hear.

The darkness of the room sets a mood
  And pace, of thoughts which abound.
As we listen, once more, and again.
  We look at this artist ply his verse,
And wonder what had inspired
  These thoughts, these words and emotions.

Do we hear the artist, or hear our inner thoughts
  As they wander about, and in and out
Amongst the words of the poet?
Do we listen to the words, so well recited,
  Or our own inner thoughts,
As we come to another reading?

Tuesday, November 9, 2004

Poems

Verses

Music ..

A Dreamer or a Poet

Amongst our midst we have a poet,
And then she exclaimed, " I didn't even know it "
He's been amongst us all our life,
Through thick-and-thin, and even strife.

He works with us, and on occasion
Some words from him escape.
Some weekend we depart to some obscure location,
And at the day's end, in conversation deep, he
begins to relate

How in his childhood, his teachers scorned
For often, during lectures ... he would dream
So at year's end, there, on report card 'Scored'
" Er ist ein Langsammer Träumer "

Now for those of you, who are in a daze,
At what those words can mean,
When at times ... at your desk ... in a haze
You sit and think . . . and perhaps you dream.

So ! . . . Are we slow ? Or deep in thought
Of what the next verse could mean ?
Just sit back ... relax ... and gather your dream
And perhaps a brand new poem, will forth be
brought.

It is best to be thought as a ' Dreamer '
As there is stigma, to the title of ' Poet '

Monday, November 15, 2004

To Wait

I Sit and ponder, to pass the time
And wait and wonder, and proceed in line
As time creeps by . . . My watch I glance
And see all others, in reposing stance.

My flight is soon,
But delay they announced
Above the Din of multitude,
So we drink another Ounce.

I sit across this bespectacled man,
His Bible in hand, he passes time,
Reading parables and verses and words of rhyme.
He also waits, the news to board
And with him also journeys the Lord.

The wheels of baggage whirr with sound
As their size, was not meant
So fast to spin round and round.
A nervous grip, their handlers grasp
Afraid the baggage should fail by the clasp.

Their journey then vexed,
Should all their contents disappear,
So they pray to the Lord
And allay their fear.

Thus patiently I sit and wait my turn
My travels to proceed for soon I shall learn,
That my wait is soon over
As I embark on my flight,
Then sit down once more
And read other people's lore.

I sleep some and read some
And share verbal trite,
With those next to me
And share conversation light.

The pilot announces our goal is just minutes away,
So we strap ourselves in again
And wait while I finish my jigger of Gin.
Then hand the glass back to the stewardess with a grin.

November 12, 2002

Crippled

This Tower is just as weak
As the lives and emotions
Of the People who have
Relied on you to supply

The light and energy which
Is transferred along your
Length of lifeline
To homes and place of work.

Crippled was their spirit, as they had become
Accustomed to the things which
Grandparents did not have;
Your light was new to them.

The patience of those in the cities
And rural points affected,
Was stretched beyond its normal duress,
For having changed their routine.

We must accept this hardship,
Which other nations find as routine.
For we have no ways to deal with this
And we clamor, and call a national disaster,

When nature throws to us in fits,
An abundance of the things,
We normally call precipitation,
Which we cannot manipulate.

These should be only nuisance,
As we are so dependant on the things,
" Contrivance " is what grandpa called,
Those fan dangled things.

Our ancestors only bade the time,
Till Gods of wind and sun would reign,
And set things right and then,
To melt and wash the land again.

Precarious is our dependence,
On things that we have come
To accept for survival, of such
What nature can deprive us.

Should we not be in position
To live in Harmony with
Nature and amenities,
As we had lived before.

The young of the last fifty years
Must learn what Grandma used to know.
Then we, as servants of this earth,
With Nature, live and flourish.

Why must disaster strike,
For us to know our neighbours?
Only then, are we to know,
That help is just a two-way street.

Come the new day on the morrow,
"Hello" should be on lips to those, we
Have not seen before,
Yet live just around the corner.

It seems that we just come across,
The parents of that young one at the pool.
When, had we looked across our yard,
They had been there, long before.

We use the crutch of work and time,
To excuse us from contact
With neighbours where we live,
For fear of making friends, and worse

Of having to rely on them, or they on you.
If ever such a storm should hit again
What would we do just then?
Pitch in and help and say "Hello,"
For we might need far more than that,

If real disaster would besiege us,
As others have known and lived through war,
Rumblings of Earthquakes or Flooding,
And shattering houses, during storm.

With such a hardship for us to bear,
Not knowing how to handle.
In Eyes of our Ancestors we do appear
A trifle to be Crippled.

October 8, 2000

Lion Seminar / Laian Seminar

We meet,
we greet
then we take a seat
and listen to speakers as we get a treat

Of stories and history of what went on
to so many people, so many long years ago,
and many of them are now, also gone.
They've moved to another homeland,

By the side of our Lord,
from age and disease
and other drawings from the cards of the Lord,
leaving family feeling and reeling and very displeased.

First one speaker and then others more,
all recalling many hundreds of scores,
of history in lands far distant from here,
and after every oration the audience sends a cheer.

Every other year the seminar is hosted by another church community
In Cities afar; so travel they do, these parishioners able to get about.
While many opt for travel in Buses, to get reacquainted with friends
Who have shared all these stories when last they had met
And they would not hesitate nor take a fret
To rekindle the contact at the very next year,
If the Lord grants that, again they will be here.

For three days we listen and three days we chat,
And from all these folks there's nary a spat.
They wine and they dine and attentively listen,
Very often we see that their eyes will glisten.

At the end of the seminar they all make a Promise
At next conference to meet again at the very next year
Only the Lord will know which will keep that Honour,
And surely all would want to be here.

Thursday, October 20, 2005

New Year 2006

May your year be worry-free, and give you time to sit under the tree;
to collect your thoughts, and to smile a lot,
while you enjoy your loved ones throughout the year,
so please; You should not shed a tear.
For after this there is another year.

So choose the right path and choose it well
and perhaps you may need to rest a Spell,
Pamper your body occasionally too
and see the gifts, from Me to You.

They certainly will not be material things
which from time to time, to you I may bring.
But certainly as I vow to you,
the sheet will have a word or two.

Will you join me in a Glass of Cheer
as we usher in, this coming Year?
Across this wide and distant land,
come greet this New Year as you raise your Hand.

Come greet this Year,
and lend an ear
to all who sorrow and shed a tear
as they just fear this coming New Year.

OH ! Did you make your wish?
And your Resolution?
Wait and see, they shortly will be here,
The things you asked and things you Yearn,
    Only the Lord will know if you Earn.

    Wishing you a Happy and Healthy New Year –
      Wünschet euch, ein Glückliches und Gesundes Neues Jahr

        Tuesday, December 20, 2005

Chapter 13: Last Voyage and Departure

A Prayer for Roma

Today I Went to a Memorial Service

Setting Sail

A Prayer for Roma

A word to share with the one above,
The Creator of life for us all,
Is asked to help us or heal us
And heal a great friend.

A prayer is shared with our Lord up in Heaven,
To help us, to heal us, to help those in need,
And now we need one, to heal our good Friend,
Our Comrade, and Brother in pain.

Pain to his family, as he suffers
An ailment, so fierce and so cruel
He needs help in his battle,
To conquer this ailment which
Gives him such pain.

With help from our Lord,
Beseeched by us all,
Our comrade may heal from this curse,
That weakens him before family and all.

Pray with us and pray for him now,
The help, which we ask for,
Is required right now, for healing is timely
And time is at prime, so pray with me dearly and waste not a moment.
Lord, help us to heal him and listen to our plea,
Give guidance to Doctors who treat him,
In easing his pain.

A prayer for Andrée, Josée and Sonia
And grandchildren too, to help them
Bear the moments, while we wait for a cure.

This prayer is asked of you, Lord,
To help us and help our friend Roma,
To heal his great pain,
This prayer is sent to You, to help one and all,
For his family needs him,
As he needs Your help right now.

We all need our good Friend
We ask you, Lord, " Please Listen to our plea. "

December 30, 2000

Today I Went to a Memorial Service

Today I went to a Memorial Service
And met the Departed's family
Today I went to a Service,
and saw the Family's new Life.
Today I went to a Service
And saw the family with Strife.

They came from near and came from far,
And some could not come at all,
As some of the family is dispersed around the world,
So they sent their message to family dear
To be read by those much nearer.

Today I came from a Service
T'was a Memorial Service
To celebrate her life's achievements,
And have the family and friends so dear,
To gather, and her past to share.

Today I went to a Service,
The Internment will take place at later date,
When all of family can attend
From all the distant lands, so dear to our departed friend.

Today we came to a Service,
To meet the new generation,
This Great Grand-Son who came to the world,
And Whose roots stem from our departed Shirley.

Today we went to a Service, to celebrate the lives of a family,
And say Adieu to a person great, and bid her "Bon Voyage"

As she sails to the House of our Lord in Heaven,
And from there be a Guide to her Family.

We bid you farewell this day so sad, and celebrate your blessings.

For Shirley Walbridge (MacAdam)

Monday, April 18, 2005

Setting Sail

Today a ship sets sail,
The Captain is alone on a journey to a destination
Far from here, as he leaves
In Mist of Sadness, and Rain of tears.

His journey is one he takes alone.
He leaves Kin, and Friends behind,
To find a port in a distant land,
Where pain and sickness cannot land.

As you wave Farewell to this lonely voyageur
Shed not too many tears,
This voyage is a trip, ordained by our Lord,
A trite bit early for our liking
As his sloop slides out of harbour.

Wave your Farewell, for his journey
As he leaves.
Shed not too many tears,
So his journey will not be rough.
To that distant port Awaiting
Where others will be waving, Welcome.

May 24, 2001

Poetry Credits, Influences and Inspiration:

" **Deanna** " is for *Deanna Harriman*, as was her Maiden name. She was the inspiration of "A *Message To A Graduate* ", my first Documented Poem.

School of Nursing was " *Livingston Hall* ", part of the *Montreal General Hospital*, where Deanna received her Nursing Degree.

"**Anna** " My Dear Sister, *Anna Meszaros*.

" **Dad** " *Peter Köhl Sr*, my Father.

" **Martin** " *Martin Meszaros*, my Nephew.

" **Patrizia** " Martin's Bride.

" **Johanna and Edouard** " *Van Ockenburg*, very Dear Friends of mine.

" **Leontine and Monique** " *Van Ockenburg*, The Children of Johanna and Edouard.

" **Pat** " *Patricia McGuigan*, Organist and Singer at **Saint-Boniface German Church** in Montreal, Qc.

" **Mary and Frank** " **Mary** and **Frank Biringer**, are dear Friends. **Frank** was a member of the Brass Band, which I was part of in the late 50's and early 60's.

"**Bonnie** " *Bonnie Wright*, dance instructor at **Dorval Social Dance Club.**

" **Bill** " *William Geiger*, Friend and fellow Band Member.

The " **Douglas** " refers to the Douglas Hospital, in LaSalle Quebec, a hospital for patients with mental difficulties.

Pictures;   **1: Author**   Reposing on Shores of Georgian Bay
             2: Roses   Photographed by Author, Cultivated
                                    in Author's garden
             3: Vase   Photographed by Author
             4: Solitary Rose   Photographed by Author
             5: **Author's Parents** Mr and Mrs Köhl
             6: Ann   Author's Sister
             7: Paddle   Author in Kayak
             8:   *Paul Brodie* -- Saxophone
                           Photo by **John Vellinga**
             9:   *James (Jim) Campbell* – Clarinet
                           Photo by **Julian Stein**, for **Festival of the
                           Sound.**
             10: Author on a Sugaring outing in Rigaud Quebec.
       Photos # 1(part) & 6 by Photographer **Marie-Andrée Robert** of
       Photolux Inc.

Sketches: of Knife and Onions, Wine Glass, Coffee Cup
          Candle, Hands and Vase by: *Rosemarie Schwab*
          of Beaconsfield, Quebec, Canada.
          (Wild–Life Artist, Illustrator and Painter - Friend and
          Neighbour)

Book Cover design by *Eclips Graphics*
     of Pincourt, Quebec.
Book Cover photo by *Peter Köhl*,
     Sunset on a road in Vermont, USA

Inspirations for Poems:

01:     ***Message To A Graduate:***   ***May 1969:***
I was asked to escort a young lady to her Graduation Ball.
She was graduating from **the School of Nursing at Livingston Hall,** part of the **Montreal General Hospital**. I wished to give an Original Gift. With a bottle of father's wine, I sat down and composed this poem, which I then had illustrated by a Calligraphic Artist, onto parchment and then framed.

02:     ***A Friend:*** ***January 3, 1995:***
Written as a Reflection on why we try to rekindle friendship and contact with people long forgotten, or the situation which caused them to relocate to another are or group of friends, thus losing contact with us. This poem is also to share with those who have stood by and supported us in our trials, and shared our triumphs.

03:     ***Kiss:*** ***September 3, 1995:***
While I was suffering the breakup of a relationship, I had a few Friends to help me through my feelings of loss, Friends of both genders with whom I could discuss the various aspects of relationships. In some of the discussions, the subject of a ' Kiss ,' with its nuances and effects, was expounded and deliberated. The poem is a compilation of these thoughts, ideas, observations and discussions.

04:     ***Sparkle:*** ***September 4, 1994:***
When I looked into Her eyes, I was inspired. It is true that ladies often say their lovers do not look into their eyes when kissing or making love. I looked and I saw sparkles in her eyes.
Gentlemen: Do you remember seeing sparkles in her eyes in your own relationship?

05:     ***Love:*** ***June, 1995:***   After much discussion with friends, Ladies and men, and of my interpretation of this VERY SENSITIVE topic, and self-analysis of my emotional failures, I wrote the following poem which I believe describes the emotion of " Love ."

06: ***Palpitations: December 19, 1995:***
This poem was purely a result of observations of reactions to a bank
teller's witnessing and mis-interpreting a glance within a situation. I
had done some transactions at the bank and there was one Service
Representative who had gone above-board, so to say, in her clearing
up some banking errors on my father's behalf with a Florida draft
which had been misappropriated somewhere. To thank this
representative for her exceptional service, I handed her a
' Thank You ' poem and her Manager was witness to this.

The manager asked if I had written other poems and in reply, I
handed to him and to the Service Representative **Beatrice,** several
poems. This **Beatrice** was of Exceptional Beauty, so I her gave a
poem called "A Kiss" (I also gave a copy to manager with a note to
give it to his spouse.) At this point in time, a teller by the name of
Rachel came over to have some document authorised and happened
to look over and see the title of the poem, "A Kiss", to which her
eyes fluttered. The manager approved her transaction and then,
huffed so as to get everyone back to work. He and **Beatrice**
thanked me for the poems and I proceeded in line to a teller to have
some other transactions cleared.
While in line, I looked over and saw **Rachel** and **Beatrice**
locking eyes, and **Rachel** motioning with the palm of her hand to
pat her chest with a nod towards me. At this moment she looked
at me as I gave a scolding motion with my finger, so she shyly gave
an apologetic look. When I got to the teller's line, I asked if she
had some Palpitations to which she responded, " NO". Later on that
evening, I wrote this poem, and the next week I handed it to
Rachel with a note of my interpretation of her Palpitations for
having read "A KISS."

The poem also applies to anyone viewing a couple kissing,
irregardless of age, encouraging them to reflect back to the times
they were in the same situation of sharing such a moment.

07: *A Rose: December 18, 1999:*
The Hesitation of buying, or not buying a Rose for a gift. Is it too early in a relationship, and then *WHICH* one to get, without being Too Emotional ? I was in this dilemma of wondering
'Is it too soon ,' for some hopeful affection? I also grow Roses of all different shades and colours in my garden.

08: *A Vase: December 7, 1996:*
If you give a Rose, you need a ' Vase ' to present it in.
Poem was a gift to **'Monique',** a friend's daughter for her 21st birthday. The Gift was a transparent hand-painted Vase into which I placed the poem I had written for the occasion.

09: *Happy Valentine: January 13, 2001:*

10: *A Smile For You Today: August 13 , 2002:*
I Thought this smile might cheer you up a little bit!

11: *Love on Valentine's Day: February 14, 2002:*
This Saint keeps getting blamed, for everything.

12: *On This Day I Wander: February 14, 2004:*
Flowers! A Card or just a Wish - which will I offer for this day?

13: *Heed Me, I do Say: December 10, 2005:*
While I was driving home from my Parents' place after having been with them and my younger Sister who was visiting from the United States, a set of verses came to my head. I repeated them so often that I would not forget them (as I could not stop on the highway to write), that when I arrived at home, I quickly jogged my faltering memory to complete this little set of lines.

14: *Saint Valentine: February 6 , 1996:*
Oh yes! One has to get some Roses or be relegated to the Dog-House.

15: *This Hand: May 23 , 2002:*
This poem was written in retrospect of what I had just lost, or never really had at all.
Was it all in my mind ?

16: *A Caress: October 9, 2000:*
Dreaming again, if only! Well I'll have to do something about it! Yes; give the poems so others can feel the emotion.

17: *Beauty: October 9, 2000:*
When one meets a Beautiful Young Woman, the mind races as well as the hormones, and one envisions much more than one can dare.

18: *A Gem: September 2, 2001:*
This one was for **Merylin,** the precious Gem.

19: *My Love, Will You Make Love to Me ?:*
March 24, 2002:
When you day-dream, you can think of a lot, and keep dreaming, or do something about it.

20: *Passion: January 28, 2001 / January 29, 2002:*
Two lovely days, and it was inspiring. Can it be repeated???

21: *Patrizia and Martin: February 17, 1994:*
My Nephew **Martin Meszaros** and his lady friend decided to get engaged.

22: *A Wedding: April, 1994:*
Oh! The Wedding ! Will I need a Tuxedo or be the
Photographer at my Nephew's Wedding ?
It is easier to be Photographer. This poem was also Translated to
Italian as his Bride and her family are Italian.

23: *Un Matrimonio: June 1994:*
Wedding poem translated to Italian, by *Kathleen Di Genova*

24: *A Birthday Comes just Once a Year: March 15, 1997:*
Written for **Maureen Geiger**, for her birthday which followed
the very next day.

25: *A Little Birdie Told Me: December 5, 2005:*
For **Susan Lindsay** of **Saturna Island, BC, Canada**. I keep
remembering those birthdays which everyone wishes to forget.

26: *Another Birthday: October 9, 2001:*
My friend Bill had his birthday so I thought about some words for
him.

27: *Is It Your Birthday Today?: May 22, 2002:*
For **Mary's** upcoming birthday.

28: *Leontine: April 11, 2000:*
For **Leontine,** this is a special wish.

29: *Dear Monique: December 7, 1996:*
One has to send wishes, as they mean a lot to the person
receiving.

30: *Fifteen: November 6, 1995:*
A young lad is to celebrate his 15th. Birthday.

31: *Johanna and Eddie: Dec 18 , 1992:*
Johanna and Eddie Van Ockenburg's 25th Anniversary:

32: **Twenty Five: *August 1994:***
Mary and Frank's 25th Wedding Anniversary:

33: ***Fifty: October 27, 1996:***
Renate's boyfriend was coming up to his 50th, so this poem is
appropriate.

34: ***Birthdays are a Number: November 7, 2004:***
Both **Frank** and my Brother **John** celebrate on the same day! A wish
for both of them.

35: ***Dear Sheelagh: January 16, 2000:***
For **Sheelagh Holden.** She did want to forget her birthday; no such
luck. I called to remind her.

36: ***New Year's Wish 2005:   January 1, 2005:***

37: ***A Thorn: March 31, 1997:***
If one is not right, nor feels right with a lady friend, then doubts may
arise. One feels like a Thorn.

38: ***A Hummingbird: August 22, 1997:***
Coming to terms with a relationship that does not seem to work!
One way of saying " Adios ". Sending a poem, was easier than
facing the person and telling her " It's over. "

39: ***The Silvery Moon: September 27, 2004 -***
December 22, 2004:
Driving to Ballroom Dance Practice in **Dorval, Quebec,** I looked
ahead of the roadway and off to the slight right in the darkened
horizon and saw the Moon, very Large and Clear. It made me reflect
on the time my love and I had Parted.

40: ***Pain: February 18, 2001:***
Reflections of why things went wrong in past relationships.

41: *The Ravages of Time: January 16, 2003:*
Birthday thoughts. We are getting older, so look into the
mirror. Before you send the message, look at yourself.

42: *How do I Speak ?: July 24, 2004:*
Not with a forked tongue! Also have your body language say the
same as the verbal one.

43: *Anger - At Me or Because of Me ?: November 7, 2004:*
Mis-understandings!
Why dance steps are not working, and tempers fray.

44: *Which is my Strength ?: November 8, 2004:*
Do we evaluate ourselves often enough? Perhaps not enough,
if ever, in the eyes of others.

45: *The Little Vampire: Monday, February 6, 2005:*
I was an unexpected patient of the Cardiac Ward of the **Jewish
General Hospital (JGH)**, and was advised that I would be a
Guest of the 5 Star * **JGH** for the weekend. On the following
Monday Morning, I would be willing (not my choice) to undergo
an Angiogram to determine why my blood pressure was Too
High and my Cholesterol was Critical. In preparation for the
Angiogram, the nurses had to take numerous blood tests
throughout the weekend, the last one at (01:00 am) Sunday
morning. While in troubled sleep, I was awakened by **Caroline**
for some more blood . . . When I came to my senses, I asked her
"Are you a Vampire?" After she completed her drawing of
blood, I composed this poem. Her reply had been "NO."

46: *Is Life A Duel ?: February 22, 2005:*
A series of Deep Thoughts of one's future after having serious
discussions with the Cardiologists. Irregardless of what setbacks
we come across, we must forge ahead.

47: *Night-Time Sounds in Room 281 D:*
Monday, February 6, 2005 :
After my Angiogram, I was not able to make too many
movements, especially bending over or folding my leg at the
groin. So sleep was as difficult as it was the night before. Again
this night, the lady in the other corner was really babbling most
of the night, so the words were born for this poem.

48: *The Day She Came to Visit: November 22, 2004:*
While visiting mother in the hospital, the lady next to her had a
very severe Hip Surgery , due to a Fall ... It was also more severe
due to her her very advanced age. The Grand - Daughter was
visiting and holding Vigil. My perception of her concern
prompted these words.

49: *Memory: January 29, 2002:*
I was inspired by the " Clients and Patients " of the **CLSC** and
of the **Liason Center** at the **Veterans Hospital**, in **Ste-Anne-
de-Bellevue, Quebec**. They had concerns and disabilities, and as
a volunteer, I was glad to be of help. This also made me think
deeply about their fears, and those of my parents who were at
times having difficulty Remembering.

50: *Friends in Music: March 22, 1997* :
These words were written after reading an upcoming shedule for
the **" Festival of the Sound "**, in **Parry Sound, Ontario**,
and reflecting on my experience of sitting enchanted and in bliss
while hearing a performance of *Srul Irving Glick's*
Hebraique Suite # 4, performed by *Valerie Tryon* on Piano and
Paul Brodie on the Alto Saxophone. This performance had
taken place the previous summer

51:     *My Glass of Wine: November 9, 2004:*
        Cleaning up after a visit by friends, the morning after
        having imbibed too much wine.

52:     *Musik Governs My Day: November 14, 2004:*
        A perfect setting to a dream I had always had, was to find a
        partner in life who is musically inclined and who can sing. A
        particular performance which influenced the words of the poem
        was **Russel Braun** - Singing, and his spouse **Carolyne Maule**
        playing Piano. This exemplifies the Ideal Musical Couple, thus
        the Poem was Born.
        As the words in the poem show (I Cannot sing).

53:     *A Pause, Tea Break or Coffee if you Please:*
              September 8, 2000:
        While busy at my desk, I missed the break, so my boss called out
        " BREAK TIME." This poem was written in response.

54:     *A Thought when Cutting Onions, or Other Slippery*
              Things: September 14, 2004:
        While I was chatting with my sister on the telephone she
        mentioned that she had just cut her fingers with the paring knife.
        Racing mind and thoughts resulted in the following poem.

55:     *Grappa: November 11, 2004:*
        If you are of European Descent, then at some point in your life
        you may have tasted this specialty. It is VERY GOOD, and has a
        very old history behind it. If not yet tasted, you may have heard
        of it from people at some occasion.

56: *Voice: October 29, 2000:*
At *Saint-Boniface* - German Church in **Montreal,** there is an
Organist, Choir Master and Singer (*Patricia McGuigan*) who sang
so beautifully (if one may use that description) that it seemed
almost like a voice from Heaven. I was so moved by the
clearness and timbre of the voice and the way it carried throughout
the Church without being loud, that when I got home, I had to put
those feelings to paper. I did print a copy of the poem for ' **Pat** '
and presented it to her the following Sunday.

57: *Music...and Song, Are a Voice in the Night:*
      August 8, 2003:
While chatting with an E-Mail friend, we talked about music and
composed a poem, A Compilation of two persons' thoughts.

58: *Cream Cheese with Bacon: September 26, 2005:*
I was sitting in a Restaurant (near the Pharmacy where I get my
medication) awaiting my breakfast order. A very attractive lady sat
beside me and ordered a different (lunch). Bagel with
Cream-Cheese and Bacon. With my Coronary Artery blockages, I
thought of how UNHEALTHY her order actually was, so I wrote
this little set of verses and presented them to her.

59: *Waffles and Waffles: February 16, 2005 / December 11, 2005:*
While enjoying Waffles at **Picasso Restaurant** in **NDG, Quebec,** I
recollected the waffles my Mother used to make in the Old
Waffle Iron and her placing this in the Flame-hole of the
Wood Stove. This reflection of By-gone days and the Waffles I was
eating now, were the Inspiration for these words.

60: ***The Sandman: October 7, 2002:***
I was sitting and recalling tales my mother told us when we were young, of the little children rubbing their sleepy eyes, yet who would not want to go to sleep.

61: ***Rain: May 2, 2005: / December 12, 2005:***
Lots of rain in a wet Spring, and we are desperately waiting for some Warmer and Dryer Weather. Rain makes one despondant and we look forward to something more Enlightening. Like maybe some *SUNSHINE.*

62: ***Retirement: September 19, 1998:***
This Poem was inspired by **Keith Ryan,** my Manager who had retired from **TransCanada PipeLines** after a transfer to **North Bay, Ontario.** Keith believed early on, that I had some skill for communicating and writing.

63: ***Quarter Century Club Party: October 6, 2000:***
A party for the workers of **TransCanada PipeLines** who had 25 years of service or more, was held in **Toronto** annually. For this year's occasion, I wrote this poem. Although I was short of the required 25 years by only six weeks, I could only go as PHOTOGRAPHER, not as a **Quarter Century Club** Member.

64: ***When I Retired I Had a Wish: December 22, 2000:***
The day of our departure from our workplace, there was no-one from management on site to bid us 'Adieu' for our service.
Three of us left on the same day, and there was no bid of farewell from Up Above. A few colleagues went with us for lunch..

65: ***Dream of the Water: July 24, 2004:***
Hot summer days make one dream of water and the sports on it, in it, or drinks made with it.

66: *Dance: November 11, 2004 :*
Thoughts of how we dance or try to, and how the other creatures of
this world do their dances.

67: *Bonnie: May 10, 2004:*
A Poem for **Bonnie Wright,** our dance instructor in
Ball-Room Dance classes in **Dorval, Quebec, Canada.**

68: *Learning to Dance: December 7, 2004:*
During my various days at dance practice and dance lessons (trying
to learn Ballrooom Dancing). I occasionaly felt
' Enough was Enough ' I needed Time-off, and did not feel like
going, so the following words are some ramblings of what goes on
in someone's (my) mind.

69: *A Paddle: August 31, 1995:*
Reflections of thoughts which **Renata** expressed when on a few
hours of a paddle on a small lake in *Adirondak Park* in upper *New
York State*, upon a visit to her old stomping areas with a side trip to
this beautiful park.

70: *Fly Fishing: September 3, 2000:*
I was Fly Fishing in a *Vermont State* river with my nephew,
swatting little Sand-flies and Mosquitos and catching my
Fishing Flies in the grasses and brush, so this poem resulted from
this and similar experiences. All Fly-Fishermen can attest to this
love; Pleasure to Some ... and Pain to Others.
        Will you get bitten by this BUG ?

71: *The Campfire Meal: September 4 - November 16, 2004:*
I was camping with my friends **Edouard van Ockenburg** and his
wife **Johanna**, and their daughters **Leontine** and
Monique (with friend Toni) at **Rollins Pond, Saranac Lake
Campground** in **New York State**. We had good times Walking,
Canoeing, Kayaking and preparing delicious meals.
The verses describe some of our antics of the weekend.

72: *My Old Cycle: December 10, 2005:*
Reflections on my adventure of learning to ride a bicycle.

73: *A Whale, She did See on the Sea: October 19, 2005:*
The inspiration was an article which **Bobbie Dunham** had
provided for the Newsletter by the **Sanctuary Cruises** of
Monterey Bay, **California**, written about her experience on a
whale watching cruise.

74: *My Brother's Old Cycle: October 23, 2005:*
Since I have stories of my cycling trials, those of my brother
were also memorable.

75: *Why do I Wait?: December 28, 2005:*
Sitting and waiting for car repairs, noises and pauses and time is
spent; then the money.

76: *Ann: March 15, 2000:*
A poem for my dear sister – **Anna**. For her Upcoming 60th
Birthday.

77: *Dad: June 18, 2000:*
A Thank You to my Father and a way of making his birthday
special. A poem written for him.

78: *The Hospital Visit -- Sequel to a Mild Stroke:*
    November 21-22, 2004:
I was Inspired while visiting Mother in the hospital after she
suffered an apparent mild stroke.

79: **_Lost on the Geriatric Ward_:**   _November 19, 2004:_
While visiting Mother in the Hospital after her fall (mild Stroke),
I noticed she had trouble expressing herself, as her speech had
been slightly affected. She asked with tears in here eyes,
" How long will I have to Stay Here?" clearly showing a fear that
we might abandon her there. The fact that there were some very
disturbed people in the adjoining rooms made her worry that she
might be in the Psychiatric Ward.

80: **_A Word:_   _October 3, 2000:_**
Rosemary Stefan: After we danced at the Folk Dance
performance, you mentioned that I use nice words, so this poem I
wrote for you.

81: **_A Light Shone from the Other Side:_**
September 9, 2000:
Thoughts and reveries while sitting in a restaurant and fixing my
attention to a burning candle, when suddenly the waitress,
Elisabeth, blew it out and broke my spell.

82: **_Poetry Reading at the Yellow Door Coffee House:_**
November 9, 2004:
Several times a year, I go to Poetry Reading sessions at the **Yellow
Door Coffee House**, the oldest one in Canada. There are readings
of Verse, Poetry and some Music, all organised by
Ilona Martonfi, in a quaint basement setting, listening to and
sharing the words of those performing. Occasionally newcomers
are invited to share some of their words.

83:     *A Dreamer or a Poet ?:   November 15, 2004 :*
While sitting and watching my wine operation, I reflected on
thecoming evening's visit to the **Yellow Door Coffee House** for
poetry reading, and thinking back on my early days of
Day-Dreaming and mind travels. Only then I did not put things
on paper, but I was thinking in the poetic lines and verses.

84:     *To Wait: November 12, 2002 :*
Waiting in the Airport for my flight to visit family back in
Germany, time passed ever so slowly as they had announced a
delay in departure. I watched the other people in various stages of
anticipation and worry as they bade the time. Writing does pass
time!

85:     *Crippled: October 8, 2000:*
I was watching a movie of disasters on television and they
recalled the ICE STORM of 1998. Upon reflection of
this ' Ice Storm ' in **Quebec** and **Eastern Ontario and in the
Northern part of North-Eastern USA,** these words came about.
It seemed very few people had an idea of how to survive in an
emergency on their own. I was lucky to have grown up in **Europe**
with VERY LITTLE but self-reliance to get us through. So these
words describe my observations of the events during and
after this Disaster.

86:     *Lion Seminar / Laian Seminar: October 20, 2005:*
The **Saint-Boniface Church** hosted the Laian / Lion Seminar this
year and the words of the poem are my interpretations of those
three days. The attending parishioners who do their utmost to be
Good Hosts to the Guests and the Invited Speakers all enjoy this
reunion and cameraderie.

87: *New Year 2006: December 20, 2005:*
Wishes to be shared with all my friends and also yours.

88: ***A Prayer for Roma: December 30, 2000:***
Roma Dostie, a colleague from work, was diagnosed with
Cancer. On this day he found out and relayed the information to his
work colleagues. This prayer was to ask for the Lord's help
to heal this friend.

89: ***Today I Went to a Memorial Service:***
Monday April 18, 2005:
For **Shirley Walbridge (McAdam)** Mother of my dear departed
friend, **Jim Walbridge.**

90: ***Setting Sail: Tuesday October 15, 2002:***
My parting words, when I assisted at **Gerhard Becker's** Funeral.
Gerry was a dear Friend and also Band Member of the Brass Band,
(**Donauschwäbische Jugend Blas-Kapelle**). **Gerry** was also a
Master Baker who supplied us with the delicious
" **Schwarzwälder Torte** ", 'Black Forest Cake' and
" **Mohn Strudel** " , ' Poppy Seed Cake.'

The poem in this book is for the Male gender. It is also written for
the occasion of a Woman's departure.

91: *Thank You: September 2, 1994:*
Written for **Beatrice,** the clerk at the Bank, who cleared up
some of the problems with my Father's Florida account. The
Original and Complete version was written for a Colleague in
Calgary (**Monika Brinck**) who assisted me on a Work Project to
get Graphics and Art-Work for a major Public Awareness
Campaign.

*It is also a fitting poem for closing remarks to
thank all people for the Friendship, Inspiration,
Guidance and source of words through my
observation.*

*May your Lord, God, Allah or Denominational
Saviour above, Guide you, Inspire you and Help you
in your choice of Words, Goals in Life and your*

" Emotions in Life "

Peter Köhl

I would like to give thanks to the **CBC**
(Canadian Broadcasting Corporation) for their
coverage of Music and Events like the Summer
Festivals such as the ' *Festival Of The Sound* ',
in **Parry Sound, Ontario**, to which I was drawn as
a result of these Broadcasts. The music aired is an
inspiration to All lovers of quality music including
myself, via Excellent Broadcasting.

A "Thank You" to **Renata Schulz** for her
excellent Piano Playing which inspired me to
develop a taste for Classical Music back in the
Mid-Sixties.

*A note of appreciation also to **Ilona Martonfi** for
her advice and help in some of my latest works.
Ilona is Producer and Host of the Poetry and
Prose Reading at the **Yellow Door Coffee House**,
on Aylmer Street in **Montreal, Quebec, Canada**.*

To All of those I say

" Thank You "

Thank You

This is oft an empty phrase.
Its meaning is to convey,
An appreciation for some
Deed performed.

It is a Favour
Being acknowledged.
A pleasure in having been performed
But still an empty phrase

How can I, with these
Scant words, convey
With so, for lack of terms
The appreciation, for your deeds?

" Danke Schön "

ISBN 142510163-1